THE

NEW

YOUTH GAMES

BOOK

ALAN DEARLING
HOWARD

WITH ILLU...   ...VILLE.

The New Youth Games Book
First Published under this title May 1994.
Parts of the book were previously published as the Youth Games Book.

Published by:
Russell House Publishing Ltd
38 Silver Street
Lyme Regis
Dorset DT7 3HS

British Library Cataloguing-in-Publication Data:
A catalogue record for this book is available from the British
Library.

ISBN: 1-898924-00-7

Typeset by Alan Dearling and Howie Armstrong
Printing by WM Print, Walsall

Russell House Publishing and the authors are grateful to Robin
Dynes and Winslow Press for use of his 'Planning Checklist' from
'Creative Games in Groupwork'.

CONTENTS

PREFACE TO THE
NEW YOUTH GAMES BOOK

It makes one seriously consider not getting out of bed to look in
the bathroom mirror, when you know you are about to go to the
office to write a new introduction to a book which was originally
compiled fifteen years before! But, here we are with a new
version of the **Youth Games Book!** Youth workers, teachers,
social workers and many book sellers have pestered us into
action. It's not just the royalty payments, honest!

For the new book, we have tried to reflect some of the changed
settings and uses in which relationship games and more general
games sequences might be used. In particular, some of the
almost 'secret' language of groupwork has been replaced with a
more plain-English approach to describing the positive and
negative aspects of games use. We have also used the
opportunity to modify a lot of the text, add and subtract a
number of games, and update many of the illustrations.

What has become apparent over the years is that whilst the book
was originally written when we were both working in youth
clubs, intermediate treatment groups and schools, in reality, the
sequences in the earlier editions of the book were often used in
very different locations. We heard from colleagues who used
material from the book for the organisation of staff training
sessions; fun and recreation in the home or pub; therapeutic work
with difficult or disturbed young people or adults; normal family
situations, at home or travelling in the car on holiday; in Romany
and New Age Traveller sites-in fact, almost anywhere adults and
young people are sharing time together.

We hope that the **New Youth Games Book** will continue to provide a source of practical stimulation for adults who want to use games as a means of developing relationships, learning and understanding with the important young people in their lives.

Finally, a few words of thanks. The 'old' book sold about 34,000 copies, so we'd like to thank all the purchasers, users and even those who liberated their copy from someone or somewhere else! Those users, together with many of our work colleagues and friends, have ensured that we keep looking for new games and diversions, and creatively question our own techniques and shopping basket of games sequences. We'd also like to say 'thanks' to our colleagues at Russell House Publishing for helping get the new book into publication, and to Jerry Neville, who we are pleased to still have on board as illustrator. Assistance with funding our research for the original book came from the Jubilee Trusts and the Scottish Office.

Alan and Howie.1994.

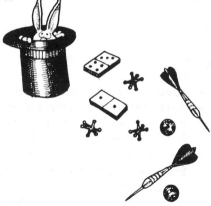

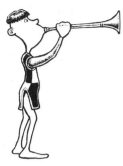

Section One:
INTRODUCTION

This is a practical book. Nobody 'owns' the games and sequences included in this book, or, rather better, they should belong to us all! The origin of many of the games is the playground, the pub or the Victorian family parlour. We have compiled this current collection with the intention of helping people who live or work with children and young people to have a toolkit of useful, enjoyable and sometimes hilarious games for sharing.

Games are seen by too many 1990's adults as something you buy from the store, wrap in gaudy paper, and distribute on Christmas Day, expecting the junior family members to go away and play with their brothers and sisters or friends. The situation is frequently repeated in schools and youth clubs, where equipment such as darts, table tennis or pool cues are lent out for use, but the adults do not share in the use.

The intention of the **New Youth Games Book** is to encourage interaction between adults and young people so that games can help those young people to:
- have fun
- develop more satisfactory relationships with peers and adults
- learn literacy and numeracy skills
- increase creativity and imagination
- improve communication skills
- cope with tension and stressful situations
- break down barriers and ease the 'getting-to-know new people' process
- identify problems and help find solutions
- build trust, sensitivity and understanding

- develop self-awareness
- develop social skills
- build confidence.

The material included in the book has been extensively used, modified and adapted to meet the needs of each particular situation. You are now part of that process! We hope that there will be a substantial number of games and sequences which will become your own for you to use as circumstances dictate. In this new version of the book, we have included some spaces for you to add your own notes on the games and add in favourites of your own.

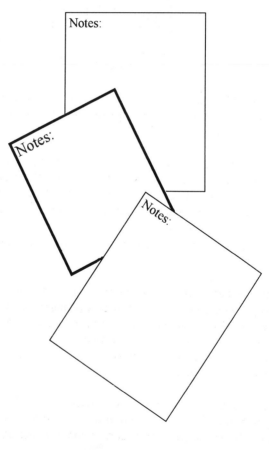

GAMES WITH GROUPS AND INDIVIDUALS

Many of the games and sequences were developed in some sort of so-called training situation. This might have been labelled a 'Social Skills' course, a youth social work group, or a classroom. Games were and are also used in what is frequently called 'Groupwork'.

Many authors and academics would have us believe that groupwork is a quasi-mystical pseudo-scientific activity, witness descriptions of groupwork, such as:

> "It is applied to situations in which social relations in specially formed groups is the medium through which social work is undertaken or where the fact and consequences of grouping make a significant difference to the objectives and approach of the work."
>
> *Timms, N & R. Dictionary of Social Welfare. Routledge and Kegan Paul. 1982.*

Lots of 'ologies' ranging from psychology, through criminology and sociology have been involved in this process of mystifying groupwork. Our view, which we hope is clear throughout this book, is that games playing and being in groups are natural and normal and do not, by necessity, need professionalising into rigid routines or a curriculum.

Nor do we rigidly treat games use with an individual as being totally separate from using a game or sequence within a group. It is frequently important for adults to make some space and time for individuals, so that they feel valued and listened to. What could be more natural than an adult showing a young adolescent a matchstick puzzle or a card trick? It is as 'normal' as telling and listening to jokes and it is the most natural environment in which learning and stimulation takes place. Where young people are especially isolated and vulnerable, perhaps because of some impairment, a bad experience, or because of social stigma, taking part in a game can break down barriers and provide an important lifeline. Games can and do provide a useful means of helping relationship-building and easing emotional hurt.

Tom Douglas, one of the gurus of groupwork rightly tried to unpick some of the myths surrounding groupwork, and his words hold true for the use of games.

> "Groups are not the prerogative of the professional helpers. They are the to be seen as a means of support and help for anyone, whether that help be in co-operation in improving facilities or the sharing of resources of knowledge, skill, sympathy, or understanding. Groupwork is not therefore a skill which can be acquired only by professionals; it can and should be learned by ordinary people to sustain them, to give them pleasure and satisfaction and their rewards of sharing in chosen aspects of their daily lives."
> *Douglas, T. Basic Groupwork. Tavistock Press. 1978.*

More recently, in his very useful compendium of games, Robin Dynes, answered his own question, "Why Games?" by saying:

> "Because they are a natural, playful means of learning and expression enjoyed from childhood...........they stimulate the imagination, make people resourceful and help develop social ability and co-operation."
> *Dynes, R. Creative Games in Groupwork. Winslow Press. 1990.*

HOW TO USE THE GAMES AND SEQUENCES

Your use of the material in the book depends greatly on why you've decided the book may be of use. If you are a parent, you may consider the book can help in strengthening your relationship with your offspring, or in extending some of their personal or social skills. Social workers, youth and community workers, probation officers and teachers are likely to find much that can be adapted to their workplace, using games for assessment; training; skills development and helping young people to adapt to change and/or deal with challenge or hurt. Trainers will find a wealth of sequences and techniques which aid participation, break the ice, and can provide exercises for individuals, pairs and large and small groups. And, as we mentioned at the beginning, games-playing is about having fun.

In the words of a famous song "Relax, and do it!"

No, we're not suggesting that you encourage a sixties-style 'be-in' or 'love-in'! The AIDS and HIV conscious 1990's certainly rules that out. We do feel that the use of games and other sequences and exercises included here requires a fair degree of 'unlearning'. Adults are naturally reticent to make a fool of themselves or to appear vulnerable. Yet, those same adults may expect young people to be 'open and honest' and unreserved.

Most of the material included needs adults to:

- feel comfortable with the material and techniques, especially the material included in Sections 2 and 4 on ice-breakers and the 'Heavy End' of relationship games.
- actively participate in the games and encourage involvement (You have to relinquish the role of observer and tutor). In other words, "Let your hair down!"
- plan group games carefully where they are part of a structured groupwork type of programme. This includes

working out aims and expectations, and involves having some sort of ongoing monitoring and evaluation procedures.
- adopt a 'horses for courses' approach which uses appropriate games and sequences for the people involved.

RELATIONSHIP GAMES

The two sections on Group Relationship Games are particularly powerful in use. They are also prone to be threatening to adults, who may see their status as being an immovable barrier to involvement. Social work managers, teachers and staff in probation and psychological services may need to learn how to cope with being put 'on the spot' by young people in a shared group situation. Parents can feel equally uneasy. Indeed, the status of being an adult frequently makes it difficult for them to operate without resort to using their power to withdraw and terminate a group experience.

If children and young people are encouraged to be truthful, open and honest and to share confidences then trust is crucial. In the context of much of the material in this collection, adults have to play by the same rules and allow themselves to be vulnerable, foolish, embarrassed. Trust is essentially based on a shared agreement. The use of the relationship games can teach adults more than a thing or two about their hang-ups, blocks and shortcomings.

We well remember being part of a large workshop at the Wembley Conference Centre. The subject was alternative lifestyles, and the organiser, Nick Alberry, co-ordinated a no-holds barred version of the 'Truth Game' which is included in this book. The workshop was operated in two smaller groups of about twenty participants. At the outset, there were about twenty adult youth leaders, teachers, social workers and the like and the same number of young people. After three days, only four adults were left and **all** the youthful participants. What had occurred was a powerful re-allocation of power to the younger members of the groups. They had found the intimate discussion and questioning about sex and relationships challenging, exciting and illuminating. Many of the adults were threatened, frightened and angry and found withdrawal from the group their only recourse. For us, it was a powerful demonstration of how a games sequence can have a lasting impact on participants and possibly unexpected outcomes.

ROLE-PLAYS AND SIMULATIONS

Being known by our occupational 'hat' or title is familiar to most adults, as is being stereotyped, rightly or wrongly, by gender, ethnic origin, religious background or sexual preference. Role-plays are a useful form of social awareness exercise, which can help young people (or older people!) to try on unfamiliar roles. The mock interview, the court session, the management committee, the TV news programme can all be 'mocked-up', especially with the greater availability of cheap and easy to handle video cameras.

Role-plays and simulations require a little more planning and preparation than many of the other games sequences included in the book. The benefits include helping participants to:

- experiment with unfamiliar roles and situations
- learn a bit more about how they and others operate in this unusual environment
- develop coping strategies to deal with similar real-life situations
- become more flexible and adaptable
- be more conscious of how behaviour and attitudes can affect those around them.

In using simulations and role-plays, organisers will often find that the sequence can generate problems as well as benefits including young people opting-out and refusing to participate, temper tantrums, scapegoating and explosive mixes of participants in the group. As in using the relationship games, it is up to the adult(s) participating to ensure that problems and emotional eruptions are sensitively confronted, rather than being ignored. This requires some skill and experience. An important element in the context of groupwork is for the group to be structured in such a way that its members share a responsibility for what goes on, and share a responsibility to resolve conflicts and problems.

Along with relationship-building techniques, role-plays and simulations will help to unlock the whole gamut of human emotions and experience. They can help take participants from 'where they are at' and constructively build on personal experience. In a small way, they can also be used to help young people to cope a little better with understanding their own selves, other people around them and the communities and societies in which they live.

Simulations have a useful place in the portfolio of game-playing, but because they are more structured and require a high level of involvement, they are generally more suited to training situations. In probation and youth social work settings we have found the types of group members are not prepared or able to give the commitment to this type of game structure. The exercises are just too complicated, and perhaps too unfamiliar. Or, maybe it's our shortcomings as games' facilitators! Either way, we have included some interesting examples which **are** suitable for staff training and senior member training in youth clubs/school social studies. Many simulations are derived from the world of management training in industry and commerce, and are extensively used in teambuilding and staff development situations. They are also used for developing communication skills and leadership models.

OTHER TYPES OF GAMES
AND GETTING THE MOST OUT OF THEM

If you've had a quick flip through the contents of the book, you'll realise that a lot of the material is not so obviously about relationship-building and social awareness. **All games** can be used as a mechanism for personal and group development, and that is why we have trawled together such a mixture of ethnic and traditional games; party games; tricks and puzzles; commercial games and activity games. Some of our categories may seem eccentric, but we have found them useful as way of dividing the types of games up in the earlier **Youth Games Book**.

Throughout the book we have offered suggestions for the use of many games, as well as describing the rules/method of play. We have also given some pointers about the potential pitfalls and advantages related to particular games and sequences.

When using any of the games it is important to consider:

- the age and gender of young people, which may be relevant to achieving a successfully functioning group
- any physical or mental impairments, such as speech impediments
- learning, numeracy and literacy skills (or lack of them) which can restrict participation in certain types of word and number games
- behaviour and attitudes of group participants, which can, if ignored, lead to bullying and oppressive behaviour
- the skills, ages, experience and attitudes of adult facilitators.

We all need praise and reassurance in order to feel of personal worth. Sharing in games-playing and group exercises can provide a forum where young people, and particularly those who are often excluded or considered difficult, troublesome or 'failures' can experience success and some sense of well-being. In this way, the sharing of a game of Mickey Mouse darts or Rotation Pool can provide an opportunity to have a positive shared experience.

A question which has recurred throughout our involvement with games is whether they should include a competitive element or not. We continue to see a place for both competitive and non-competitive games, as long as winning is not seen as the only positive outcome. A lot of life is competitive, and both the authors have enjoyed taking part in sports and games which have 'winners'. We cannot see anything intrinsically wrong in offering some games which will produce win and lose situations, as long as the taking part and sharing enjoyment are equally important. As a balance, we have also included non-competitive and trust sequences, which are designed to foster individual and group co-operation and cohesion.

Elsewhere, we have tried to remind anyone using the book that **play should be part of all our lives**. Many adults have forgotten how to play. This is not meant as an insult, rather it is stating the obvious. To return to 'play' often requires the adult to 'unlearn' much of their adult consciousness. Many of the ethnic games from jacks and fivestones, through darts and cards, and the puzzles and

two-player games and tricks lead to a "Oh, yes, I remember that!" response from adult participants. Well and good, and a useful step on the route to re-learning how to enjoy creative play.

We have also tried to include a variety of tricks, and lateral thinking tests which provide a simple opportunity for young people to learn a skill and then gain some social benefit from that knowledge, through being able to demonstrate their new found skill. Without repeating ourselves too often, **participation** is the key to the successful use of games. This is especially important in using commercially produced games, which do tend to be given as presents, or handed out as 'equipment', rather than utilised as a sharing   of   experience. In almost any type of work with young people, it can often be the informal chat which can have the most lasting impact, whilst on the surface engaging in a totally different activity, such as games playing. Adults responsible for bringing up children, whether they are parents or care workers in a children's home, sometimes have to remind themselves that it is only too easy to find excuses for why they do not spend 'free' time with the children or young people. Don't worry, we're both guilty as well!

We would also like to point games-users towards remembering the wide variety of **situations and places** where some of the games could be used. These include:

- colleges and universities
- social work and probation groups
- fetes, fairs etc.
- play groups
- adventure playgrounds
- playschemes
- after-school clubs
- school playgrounds
- schools
- sports facilities
- youth clubs
- the home
- residential centres
- on holiday
- in cars, trains, planes, buses etc.
- training events
- conferences
- cafes, pubs etc.
- counselling sessions and therapy
- hospitals

We have also included a special section on work with groups of younger children. This, once again could be useful for parents or playgroup leaders organising a children's party, or for social groupworkers. Some of the Activity Games and sequences from other sections, such as Section Two: Icebreakers, are particularly good for younger groups who thrive on action and the opportunity to let off steam!

At the end of the book is a bibliography, which like all other resource lists is our own personal 'best guess' of materials and sources which you may find useful, and which have served our purposes over the years very well.

AND FINALLY

We do hope that you find this collection useful. We still have fun using the games and sequences, but freely own up to our own inability to remember half of what we've included! So, like you, we have to put the book and our notes in our bags anytime we go off for a games-session! We enjoyed the collating, re-writing, learning about new games sequences, and testing (playing with!) the material. Always plan your sessions if you are working in a groupwork environment. Be much more flexible and informal if you are using the games material with family and friends. Most of all, enjoy yourselves and do let us know if you are using games which you would like to share with us. Also, if you feel confused by any of the material, we'd better know about that as well!

To contact us, write to
Alan Dearling and Howie Armstrong
c/o Russell House Publishing
Russell House
Lym Close
Lyme Regis
Dorset DT7 3DE

Section Two: GROUP GAMES AND ICEBREAKERS

RELATIONSHIP GAMES

Relationship games are used to promote personal growth and development, and to help groups of people who are new to one another build trust and healthy relationships more quickly than would otherwise be the case. They are used extensively by youth workers, social workers and other professionals in a variety of contexts with young people and adults.

Relationship games are qualitatively different from the games discussed elsewhere in this book. Although there may be a high gaming or fun element in them, their use with a group of people is intended to help individuals acquire the skills which will enable them to communicate and relate better to others. The use of a particular game may be intended to:

- increase self-confidence
- encourage constructive criticism of self and others
- build up and expand social skills
- or foster self-awareness.

And as a by product they may encourage literacy and numeracy as well.

Many of the games and sequences in this section and the 'Heavy End' (Group Relationship Games, Section 4) started life from a diverse range of backgrounds as 'street games', training exercises or dramatherapy techniques. However, quite a number were then 'hi-jacked' and 'professionalised' by many social groupworkers who claimed them as psychometric-behaviour modification-social engineering tools! We would like to see many of these games return to 'ordinary' situations like the streets, youth clubs and classrooms. They are too useful (and enjoyable!) to remain hidden behind the closed doors of formal groupwork or therapy sessions.

All of the games have an element of individual risk-taking or disclosure in them; this might involve physical contact with peers and adults, miming in front of the group, or making personal statements about a group member. The point about risk-taking and personal disclosure is that these are the mechanisms which help people to build relationships with one another.

If you think of some of your own valued **personal relationships,** you'll discover that they are important because of the degree of trust which has been built up through shared experiences. You'll also notice that you can discuss almost anything with your closest friends, because personal risk-taking and disclosure has become an integral and accepted part of the friendship. Relationship games help us to discover the 'real people' within us, rather than the 'work' or 'personal stereotypes' we usually present to the world.

Relationship games can be used in any situation where you would normally use games. They are a particularly powerful tool when used regularly within a group - whether this is a family group, a youth club, or a professional group which aims to produce attitude and behaviour change among its members. And, very importantly, some of them make superb party games!

To be used effectively, relationship games require more preparation than simply making sure that you have the right materials to hand - the essence of this lies in:

- making sure that there is sufficient mutual trust and confidence in the group to enable individuals to take risks without feeling unduly threatened
- matching the particular qualities of a game to the stage of development of a group and the individuals within it.

These preparation skills will develop with experience, and if you begin to run games sessions (as distinct from simply using the occasional game) you will want to utilise games drawn from several sections of this book. Robin Dynes' excellent checklist from 'Creative Games in Groupwork' is reproduced at the end of this section as an aid to preparing games sessions.

There are a few other points about relationship gaming that we want to stress. In the introduction we highlighted the fact that adults often have to re-learn the skill of playing games - this is critical when using relationship games, particularly the 'Heavy End' (Chapter 4). Adult members of the group must 'play the game' by participating fully and honestly, thereby putting themselves on an equal footing with other group members in terms of risk-taking and personal vulnerability. Without this quality of commitment to the games from adults, the group is likely to become disillusioned and slip (quite rightly!) into an 'us and them' stance. Older adolescents in particular can often be encouraged to play on the grounds that adults will be participating on exactly the same basis as they are. Quite right too!

The working through of **feelings** generated by the games must also be planned for. In the advanced version of the 'COMPUTER' game, for example, a player may have to read aloud a card which states that she is:"**THE PERSON WHO HURTS OTHER PEOPLE'S FEELINGS MOST OFTEN**". Feelings generated in this kind of game cannot be left hanging in the air; they must be discussed during the game itself, immediately afterwards, or in a separate discussion setting.

If you are using relationship games in a work setting with young people, it is sensible to organise some kind of **training session** where adults can participate in playing, organising games sessions and introducing games. This also serves to familiarise adults with some aspects of the games that they may find initially threatening. Experience of this kind will help adults build up a repertoire of skills that will help them to share the tasks of introducing and organising games. Eventually, this can be shared with young people in the group when they have gained experience of playing particular games.

The playing of relationship games is very much a private group experience and young people cannot be expected to 'lay themselves on the line' in a situation where there are constant interruptions or where non group members are likely to be watching them.

Relationship games can be successfully used with a **wide range of young people,** although the greatest benefit will be experienced by those who are under stimulated and/or lacking in self-esteem and confidence. In working with this kind of group it should be remembered that young people experiencing this kind of difficulty will 'present' it in a variety of ways; one may be aggressive and challenging with adults and peers, while another may be quiet and withdrawn. Wherever possible, workers should take the opportunity of planning group membership to ensure a balance of personal qualities and social skills. Care must also be taken in preparing material that matches the literacy and numeracy of group members, otherwise there is a danger of alienating participants.

Particularly with young people whom you do not know well, there is the danger of triggering deep-seated emotions or issues which would not normally be disclosed. You need to have strategies for dealing with this kind of situation should it arise, such as - stopping the game and moving into a one-to-one or a small group to discuss the issue, 'holding' the issue for discussion in a later session, or by providing specific support for the young people affected.

Finally, we want to reinforce the concept of 'gaming', and relationship gaming in particular, as one small move towards reinstating the sense of community which has been lost to many of us over the past 15 years. Relationship Games can be incredibly powerful in use and tend to encourage deep and healthy relationships together with a sense of true community spirit and collaboration amongst those who share in their playing.

ICEBREAKERS

We use this selection of Icebreakers heavily in introductory sessions, but would also use many of them throughout the life of a group. Icebreakers are used to 'set the scene' for relationship games and other group activities. Many of them are quite physical or energetic, and are suited to getting rid of excess energy prior to relationship gaming or more sedate group activities.

In a similar vein, they can be used to energise (i.e.waken up!) the group after discussion sessions or similar. It's common to use two or even three short Icebreakers at the beginning of a games or activity session - always try to have 'something up your sleeve' in case the group consumes your two carefully prepared Icebreakers in three minutes flat!

It is crucial to select games that the group is comfortable with, especially in introductory sessions. You should be aware by now that we look on any game or technique as potentially useful or adaptable. The crux is that they should meet the needs of the group and be simple to play. Icebreakers and the Heavy End should not be viewed as mutually exclusive categories, but as the building blocks of a relationship games session which might also include activity games, New Games etc.

The **Planning Checklist** which follows - together with our comments on individual games, sequences and exercises - are intended to stimulate an awareness in the reader of both the adaptability of relationship games and their complexity.

Playing times are offered for rough guidance only - we have known some games, e.g. Truth, Double Dare, to last for hours - others can 'burn out' in minutes with some groups. As a general rule of thumb, try to finish games while there is still interest and enjoyment around. Groups will tend to want to repeat positive experiences and will build up a repertoire of games which are important and enjoyable to them.

PLANNING CHECKLIST

1   Be enthusiastic.

2   Plan the session.

3   Give thought to the sequence of games; make sure there is variety - follow an inactive game with something active.

4   Take into account the needs of group members and their ability to interact with eachother.

5   Be aware of the players' ability to concentrate. Adapt games so that they are challenging but do not run too long - games can be lengthened or shortened.

6   Choose games suitable to the size of group and the space available for the activity.

7   Adapt the games to make them interesting to suit ages, interests, abilities and so on.

8   Make sure you are familiar with the game and can explain it easily.

9   Do not keep people waiting.

10   Introduce the game in a manner which sets the tone and explains why it is being played.

11   Do any preparation before starting the game. Have all the materials to hand. There should be no long gaps while you run out to photocopy something or decide what to do next.

12   Be prepared to act as a role model and take part in the game.

13   Do not be a know-all!

14   Repeat and clarify instructions for those who did not hear or understand.

15   Give plenty of praise and encouragement.

16   Assist individuals who are having difficulty to participate.

17   Sense the changing moods of the group while playing and vary the programme accordingly, perhaps by changing the tempo, including an extra game or staying with something they find interesting and leave something else out.

18   Respect the players' right not to share feelings, emotions and private information about themselves.

19   Have a sense of humour.

20   At the end of the game or session, summarise what has been achieved and discuss as necessary. If the game is purely for enjoyment this can be done by showing interest in whether or not people enjoyed it.

21   Keep a record of each session and how each game went. This can be used to plan future sessions.

(Taken with grateful thanks from 'Creative Games in Groupwork' by Robin Dynes). (Winslow Press).

THE BALL GAME ✎

This is the 'standard' name game which can be used with any age group. It's more fun with large numbers and there are a number of variations which make the game slightly more difficult.

The game leader asks the group to stand in a circle and explains that throwing a softball or football around is going to help the group memorise each other's names quickly. The rules of the game are outlined: "When the football is thrown to someone, they catch it, say their own name out loud and then throw the ball to any other member of the group, who must then say their own name and throw the ball on to someone else."

The game benefits from being played at a brisk pace, and the leader will therefore encourage this. Once a good rhythm and pace have been set up, the game can continue for several minutes, until the leader feels that people have had a chance to familiarise themselves with each other's names. At this point a variation can be introduced. This calls for people to state the name of the person they are going to throw the ball to, prior to throwing it.

Further rule changes can be introduced, e.g. not allowing any person to pass the ball twice to the same person, or only allowing passes to people of the opposite sex. Prior to introducing some of these more difficult rules, the group's memory can always be refreshed by playing a few rounds of the original Ball Game. Playing time: 5-10 minutes depending upon the size of the group. Can be used in an initial session with the 'Hello Game' and 'Criss Cross Naming' or 'Card Pairs'.

HELLO GAME

This is especially useful for groups which are meeting together for the first time, and can be used with any age group. The game will work best with a largish group.

You will need a set of prepared action cards which name people in the group. A card might say 'Blow a kiss to Mary' or 'Shake your fist at Bill'. It is important that cards are made up for each person in the group, and this necessitates knowing who will be coming along to the session. (Cards will have to be removed for anyone who does not turn up.)

It is usual in this kind of game to play two or three rounds, giving each person several opportunities to pick a card. About 30-45 cards would therefore be needed for a 15 strong group. In this case the game would last around 20 minutes to half an hour.

The game is played with everyone sitting in a circle while the leader explains that the aim of the game is to help people get to know each other's names. The pile of cards can be placed in the centre of the circle, or can be held by a member of the group. This will be decided by the game leader who might want to encourage someone to play by asking them to hand out the cards.

The game leader asks for a volunteer to pick the first card, read it out and perform the action. The first volunteer, (probably an adult), will show initial confusion at not knowing who Mary is; this can be overcome by, e.g. asking someone in the group if Mary is the one with the red or black hair, or by addressing all the girls in the group until he finds Mary.

This is a co-operative game, and the leader should encourage players to offer advice to each other. Can be used in an initial session along with 'The Ball Game' and 'Criss Cross Naming' or 'Self Introductions'.

SELF INTRODUCTION

This is another useful getting-to-know-each-other sequence that can be used, for instance, at the beginning of a new group, at a training meeting, or at the beginning of a new school class.

The facilitator gets everyone who is participating to form into a circle. They are then given a number, starting with number one for the group organiser. Once everyone has a number, the facilitator calls out **two** numbers between one and the highest number in the circle. If it is two and ten, the facilitator says:"Two meet Ten!" The two people with the corresponding numbers move into the centre of the circle and give their names to the other person and more generally to the group. This sequence continues until everyone has been introduced at least once. The person organising the sequence must remember to call their own number!

CARD PAIRS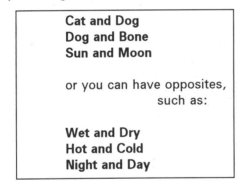

For this sequence, the person in charge of the group needs to prepare sets of cards or slips of paper in advance. The idea is to prepare a number of pairs of cards which will provide an amusing way of getting people to get to know one another. Write one word on each card. The pairs of cards can really be anything, but must be fairly easy to recognise, such as:

> **Cat and Dog**
> **Dog and Bone**
> **Sun and Moon**
>
> or you can have opposites,
> such as:
>
> **Wet and Dry**
> **Hot and Cold**
> **Night and Day**

MUSICAL INTRODUCTIONS

Yet another way to get to know other group members comes from dramatherapy via an Aberdeen Youth and Community Work student on placement in Dundee. You can't get a much more convoluted introduction than that! The sequence is suitable for any age group and works well with groups of between 10 and 20. A reasonable amount of space is required since, as in musical chairs, you are requesting that participants jump, skip and dance their way around the room in time (?!*!) with the music.

The organiser, who has an itchy finger poised over the pause button of a cassette recorder, instructs the group as to which part

of their body should touch the floor when the music stops.
Imagining yourself as the organiser, you might say: 'right hand',
or, 'left knee', or, 'nose'. As soon as the music stops, the players
all drop down onto their right hand, or whatever. Whoever is
judged to be last is told to introduce themselves to another player
and learn that person's name in return. They then join hands for a
quick bound round the room, as the music recommences.

This time it might be last person to touch 'bottom to floor'.
Remember that those joined together must try to do the exercises
'together' if possible. Again, the last down is told to join the
original twosome and introduce themselves. As the 'line' gets
bigger, the leader can split the line into smaller units for ease of
'introductions'.

This sequence can continue until all have been 'last down'.
Strangely for this sort of game, those who succeed in remaining
'in' feel outsiders, not having been introduced to any other players.

GROUP SORT

This is a good way to start a session with a group of half a dozen
people or more. The idea is to instruct the group to sort
themselves out into a single line by some factor such as age,
height or the alphabetical order of their christian names. So, in a
group of eight, Alan might be at the front, Angus next, then
Catherine, followed by Debbie, then Howie, etc, right along to
William at the end of the line.

Variations could be shortest at the front ranging through to tallest
at the back, or, youngest at the front and oldest at the rear of the
line. The game can get youngsters to begin talking to one another,
and in moving around and chatting, relationships develop and
tensions begin to subside. A couple of sequences, in a group of
ten, takes 7-10 minutes.

SHOUT

This is a fine co-operative experience which requires some
concentration to work properly. It can be used with any age group

and with both large and small groups. The group can be either standing or sitting in a circle.

The leader requires a volunteer to act as 'cheerleader', and points out that this person will have to choose a word and whisper it to the group, who will whisper it back. The cheerleader then says the word again, but slightly louder this time, and again it is repeated by the group in unison. The sequence continues until people are yelling as loud as they can.

The role of the cheerleader is very important, as the sequence works best if it builds up gradually to a crescendo. It is often a good idea for an adult to demonstrate this, by volunteering to be 'cheerleader'.

The sequence can be made more sophisticated by reversing it when the crescendo has been reached, so that the 'shouts' become quieter and quieter until they can hardly be heard. Once the group is acquainted with the full sequence a variation can be played where the cheerleader operates a 'volume control'. In this case the cheerleader controls the volume non-verbally by signalling to the group whether they want more or less volume. A suitable method of signalling should be demonstrated by the games leader.

Playing time will depend on the number of people who want to try being a cheerleader. It is rarely the case that everyone wants to, and adults in the group should be prepared to encourage people to have a go. With this kind of repetitive sequence it is best to limit the time spent on it to a maximum of 10 minutes or so. 'Shout' can be used as a lively introduction to completely different sequences like the 'Word Association Game' or 'Buzz'.

TOUCH

This sequence can be used to introduce physical contact to the group. It uses the same clapping rhythm as the 'Word Association Game' and can be followed by it quite easily or by one of the physical trust games, like 'Passing the Person'. The sequence can be used with most age groups but is best suited to a largish group.

The clapping rhythm is very important and the leader should ask the group to practice this first, perhaps before explaining the rest of the game. Try a clap-clap-space rhythm, and explain to the group that in the spaces, group members have to touch the person on their left, and then on their right alternatively.

Once this rhythm has been successfully established for a few minutes, the leader can stop the sequence and explain that a different bit of the body must be touched each time - head, toe, arm, hand, etc. The game should be stopped when the group has run out of suitable bits of body! Playing time about 5-10 minutes .

PASS THE SQUEEZE

A guessing game which can be used along with similar ones like 'Guess the Leader'. It can be played with most age groups and works best with largish numbers. Usually played standing (or sitting) in a circle, the aim of the game is for the person in the middle to guess where the squeeze is.

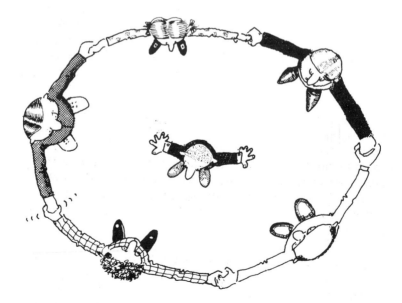

The leader should ask a volunteer to stand in the centre of the circle and ask the rest of the group to hold hands. The leader should explain how the squeeze is passed round the circle i.e. if someone's left hand is squeezed, then that person squeezes the hand which is held in their right and so on round the circle. It is often worth having a couple of 'dry' runs, so that the group get the idea - try asking them to pass the squeeze as quickly as possible. The squeeze commences with the volunteer turning their back to the person nominated by the leader to pass the squeeze.

This person can now pass the squeeze to their left or right. The person in the middle should be told to shout 'Stop!' when they know where the squeeze is. Immediately after shouting 'Stop!', the person in the middle must name the person they think has the squeeze. If the guess is correct, the two swap places, the person with the squeeze becoming the new person in the middle and the other starting off the new sequence. If the guess is incorrect, the person in the middle should be allowed two more guesses before being replaced by another volunteer.

To keep the sequence going at a brisk pace, the leader should encourage people in the middle to use their guesses fairly quickly, and should discourage group members from stopping the squeeze on its journey round the circle (perhaps to fool the person in the middle, or even just for the hell of it). Allow 10-15 minutes playing time.

CHOO CHOO

This little exercise in getting to know everyone in a group is also known as the 'Train Game'. It is quite the silliest introductory session we know and is ideal for all ages and groups of about 10 and over. Because it amuses the spectators - those not yet involved, it can be used in the context of organising events on a quite grand scale.

The game's organiser (that's you) gets the group into a circle facing inwards. Then you start off the sequence saying, "My name is Alan, (or whatever) I am a train, choo-choo ..." A good way of accompanying these verbals is to make train-like movements of an

old puffer, chugging your way up to one of the bemused
onlookers. At this point they may have a wee fit of hysterics, or
whatever, as you ask them their name saying: "My name is ....,
what's your name?" Getting the reply, for instance, Jane, you then
say "Her name is Jane, her name is Jane, choo-choo," while
swinging out your right leg and arm in unison first, followed by the
left counterparts. The recipient of this wonderful greeting joins on
the front to form a two-person train, and off it goes, 'choo-
chooing' round the circle picking up more names and bodies. It's
great fun and an ideal smile manufacturer!

BUZZ

A diabolically simple game in concept, 'Buzz' brings out
mathematical skill in the unlikeliest of people. It can be used with
most age groups in a large or small group format. There are a
couple of variations - the basic sequence can be used as a quick
'taster' before moving on to the others.

The game is played sitting in a circle. The leader explains that it
involves counting one at a time around the circle e.g., 1, 2, 3, 4,
5, etc., except that when the number 7 is reached the person says:
'BUZZ' in substitution for the number 7, or multiple of 7 (14, 21,
28 etc.), or a number with a 7 in it (e.g.17, 27, 72 etc.). The
leader must nominate someone to begin the sequence, by asking
them to start with any number between 3 and 6, the numbering
going clockwise. So the sequence should go 5, 6, BUZZ, 8, 9, 10,
11, 12, 13, BUZZ, 15, 16, BUZZ, 18, 19, 20, BUZZ, etc.

Once the group have got the hang of this, the leader can introduce
a new rule - the direction of numbering round the circle will change
at each BUZZ, thus livening up the game considerably! The game
can be played where players are out if they make a mistake but
this can often lead to most people being out within a couple of
minutes! It's a good idea to play several quick rounds without this
rule, to build up the group's collective skill, before bring in
elimination.

A further variation involves adding FIZZ (multiples of 5 and
numbers with a 5 in them) to BUZZ. So a round might go: 4, FIZZ,

6, BUZZ, 8, 9, FIZZ, 11, 12, 13, BUZZ, FIZZ, 16, BUZZ, 18, 19, FIZZ, BUZZ, etc. By the time you reach 35, because it includes a multiple of 5 and 7, this is 'FIZZ BUZZ'. Allow about 20 minutes or so.

RING ON A STRING

This guessing game, which is similar to 'Pass the Squeeze', is best played in a large group. The leader should have to hand a large loop of string with a ring on it. The loop of string should be big enough to be held by players behind their backs, when they are standing in a circle formation.

A volunteer is required, whose job it is to stand in the middle of the circle and guess where the ring is. The ring, of course, is passed from person to person around the circle behind their backs. The leader should stress that the group needs to 'fox' the person in the middle by keeping their hands moving and faking passes of the ring. When the volunteer thinks they know where the ring is, they should shout 'stop', and make a guess. If this is correct, they swap places with the holder of the ring, who becomes the next person in the middle.

To start the game off, the leader should ask the volunteer to face away from a nominated person who will start the ring on its way round the circle. The leader must decide on the number of guesses allowed - three is a good number the first time the game is played; experienced groups can be limited to one. If a person's guesses are all incorrect, the leader will have to nominate someone in the middle or ask for a volunteer. Some youngsters (and adults too) may have genuine difficulty in working out where the ring is - in this situation the leader should strongly encourage guessing, to prevent possible embarrassment to the person in the middle and to maintain the pace of the sequence.

Playing time should be limited to a maximum of 10-15 minutes. 'Ring on a String' can be played as an enjoyable set with other guessing games e.g. 'Who Am I?', 'Guess the Leader'.

KILLER

A very popular trust game with plenty of opportunity for amateur dramatics! It's best suited to a large group, and is played sitting in a circle. A little advance preparation is required, as one 'Killer' must be randomly chosen for each round of the game. This can be done by passing a piece of paper to each group member, with a cross on one piece denoting the killer. Alternatively, the person introducing the game can use playing cards, one for each member of the group, denoting, say, the Ace of Spades as the killer card.

Players should be instructed to look individually at their card or piece of paper, without letting anyone else see it. The stage is now set - there is a killer in the room, but no-one (except the killer) knows who it is. The killer kills by winking so make sure that there is opportunity for good eye contact between group members. The rules of the game are quite simple:

1. The killer tries to kill as many people as possible before being discovered. You kill someone by looking directly at them and winking once.
2. Anyone on the receiving end of a wink is dead, and out of the game, but must wait a few seconds before 'dying' dramatically. This is a crucial rule and must be strictly adhered to, as it increases the killer's chances of remaining undetected and therefore tends to prolong the game into its more exciting stages where people are dropping like flies and panic begins to set in!
3. Anyone, at any time can make a guess at the killer's identity. If the guess is correct, the killer must own up, and a new round begins. If the guess is incorrect, the person who made it must die (dramatically if possible) and the game continues.

Killer is a good shared experience and helps build confidence in individuals. Considerable status can be obtained by being a good killer, not to mention the kudos gained from portraying a histrionic death. Allow 20-30 minutes.

PEOPLE

Basically a 'silly' game, it nonetheless introduces the group to the idea of labelling individuals with particular attributes. It can also involve some spontaneous miming and is probably best used with a large group of under 15s.

A set of funny 'people' cards is required, one for each person in the group. Cards will be along the lines of 'Michaelangelo', 'Kermit', 'Hot Lips', 'Tarzan' etc. The leader will start the game by nominating someone to take a card from the pile and asking them to give it to the person he thinks it suits best! - without saying what is on the card.

That person keeps the card, chooses one themself and gives it to the most appropriate person, and so on until each person has one card only.

The leader now asks the group to introduce themselves to each other, starting with the person who took the first card, who might give a typical Tarzan yodel and say "I'm Tarzan". The sequence continues around the circle until everyone has introduced themselves. The leader can suggest doing the introductions again, but this time with some mime appropriate to each character. Playing time: about 20 minutes.

WORD ASSOCIATION GAME

This sequence can get people working together really well as a group, and is great fun to play, especially with large numbers.

The game puts people 'on the spot' in a mock-threatening way, and by its insistence on equal participation from all, helps to build up confidence in individual group members.

The leader should get the group to sit in a circle and practice a clapping rhythm, e.g. clap-clap-space, before explaining that in the spaces people have to say out loud around the circle a word connected to the one that has just been said by their neighbour.

A volunteer is needed to say the first word, with the person on, say the right, then having to give a related word. So a round might go: **clap-clap house, clap-clap garden, clap-clap hose, clap-clap water etc.**

Once the group is familiar with the sequence, it can be played with the stipulation that anyone who fails to get their word in before the 'clap-clap' sounds again is out. It is also possible to challenge players if e.g., someone thinks that a word does not have an association with the previous one. Other rules can be added, like not allowing a word to be repeated in any one round, or not at all.

It is usual to play several rounds of the basic sequence before tightening up on the chosen rules and playing it on a competitive basis. Watch out for words like xx! or xxx!! slipping in to test out adults' personal boundaries. The Word Association Game can be played for up to 20-25 minutes.

PASSING ON OBJECTS

This is a simple and often hilarious miming sequence which can be used with any age group to encourage imaginative responses to mime situations. It doesn't require a lot of people and can therefore be used as a family introduction to miming skills. Any number can participate, and it should be noted that adult involvement is crucial in providing a variety of miming models which youngsters can copy and adapt. This sequence should be used with large inexperienced groups only when there are several adults around to participate and offer encouragement and guidance to other players.

The basic technique involves the group sitting in a circle and passing an imaginary object to each other round the circle. The sequence will normally start with the games leader or someone nominated by them. Good objects to pass are things like; sticky chewing gum, a heavy rock, a pet rabbit, etc. Try to make sure that the person starting the sequence off is able to mime imaginatively and can encourage their neighbour to accept the object in a way appropriate to the mime. This process can be helped by other adults in the group, who should feel free to encourage the group to 'tune in' to the mime by commenting, "What is that?", "It must be something really sticky" or "I wouldn't like to have that passed to me in the dark!"

Each object should pass completely round the circle before the leader asks for another volunteer or nominates someone to start off a new object. When using the basic technique, the objects should be 'known' either by the leader stating that e.g. a heavy rock is about to be passed round the group, or by the person starting the sequence picking a card and reading it out. A prepared set of 5 or 6 cards should be enough before moving on to other variations.

Variations:

The first one involves asking the group not just to pass the imaginary object, but to do this while pretending to be a particular kind of person, e.g. policeman, old lady, social worker, delinquent, etc. So, the whole group could act as e.g. old ladies, or individuals could be selected to role play different characters, perhaps by distributing prepared cards with a character on each one.

The second variation involves each person changing the object received into something else before passing it on. Someone might receive a piece of sticky chewing gum and 'mould' it into a teapot before passing it on. Again, adult involvement IS important in encouraging the group to work out what each new object is, and perhaps whether the mime could have been more successful if done in a different way.

While the basic sequence is fairly simple, the variations are quite demanding and should be gradually introduced to the group over several sessions. About 15 - 20 minutes should be allowed for each sequence. 'Passing on Objects' can be used as a good introduction to 'Clay Modelling' or 'People'.

GET KNOTTED!

Although essentially a small group physical experience, this game has great spectator value, so it can easily be played by different combinations of 6 to 8 people from a larger group.

This is one of many contact experiences which help young people of all ages get used to the idea of physical touch and expression. In a small group situation, the leader would be expected to participate in the experience with the whole group but this is not crucial in a larger group where a 'director-type' role can be used.

The sequence requires one of the 6 - 8 players to leave the room or turn away while the rest 'Get Knotted'. They do this by standing in a circle holding hands and then tangling themselves up by (still holding hands!) crawling between legs, stepping over linked arms, etc. When they are well and truly knotted, the remaining player attempts to untie them, (without using violence!) and with the others still holding hands. You'll be surprised how difficult it can be.

The sequence can be repeated several times and may last for 15 minutes or so. Contact experiences like this one can be used together as a series to finish off a session in an enjoyable way.

ARMADILLO

Confusion is the end result of this sequence and is perfectly in order, as 'Armadillo' comes into the category of 'silly' games! Although it can be played in the small group setting, it is tremendous fun in a large group. 'Armadillo' is a passing sequence, so the person introducing the game should be equipped with a small object like a pen or pencil and ensure that the players are seated in a circle. The sequence goes like this:

The person nominated to start the sequence (Player 1) takes the pen and passes it to the person on their right, saying "This is an Armadillo!". Player 2 asks Player 1 "What is it?" and Player 1 repeats "It's an Armadillo". Player 2 now passes the pen to the person on their right (Player 3), saying "This is an Armadillo!" Player 3 asks Player 2 "What is it?", Player 2 then asks Player 1 "What is it?", and Player 1 states to Player 2 "It's an Armadillo!" Player 2 states to Player 3, "It's an Armadillo!", thus giving Player 3 a reply to his question. Player 3 can now pass the pen to Player 4, stating "This is an Armadillo!"

If you have read this carefully (and have an I.Q. of 140+!) you'll have worked out that when a player receives the pen, the question "What is it?" must be repeated anti-clockwise around the group until it reaches Player 1, whose reply "It's an Armadillo!" must pass clockwise all the way back to the player with the pen before they can pass it on. Eventually, with a bit of luck, the pen finds its way back to Player 1.

'Armadillo' is a lot easier to play than it is to explain, so give it a try with the group after the minimum of explanation, and give advice to players as the game continues. Once the group have got the hang of it, the **full version** can be played. This involves Player 1 starting the sequence as before, and then immediately passing another pen or pencil to the left, stating "This is a Hippopotamus!" There's a fair chance that when the 2 objects meet in the middle of the group, the sequence will collapse in jovial confusion!

Most groups will want to try the sequence again and this should be encouraged but adults should resist any temptation to press the group into 'doing it correctly', as the concentration required for this will often come spontaneously, as players become 'hooked' by the sequence.

Good for building verbal confidence and aiding concentration, 'Armadillo' can often entertain a group for up to half an hour. Incidentally, we are informed by Susan Cross that this sequence is sometimes known under the name 'Schmoos and Ardvaarks'. Susan works for an organisation whose new name is so ludicrously long that we hesitate to mention it (NCH Action For Children Scotland!)

ESCAPE/OUTSIDER

This is a good rough and tumble contact exercise for most ages, which is best used with largish groups. There are several variations which involve a volunteer breaking into, or out of a circle formed by the rest of the group.

Considerable frustration can be experienced by the volunteer, who must confront the collective strength of the group. The sequence can therefore be used to stimulate discussion around the areas of frustration and alienation.

If the exercises are to be used as a lead-in to discussion, this should be stated by the leader who should ask the group to concentrate on their feelings as they go through the exercises. Discussion can focus on questions like: "How would you describe your behaviour during the various exercises?", "Which exercises did you like/dislike the most, and why?", "What feelings did you have for people in the group as you went through the exercises?"

The **basic sequence** begins with the group standing in a circle with linked arms, and the volunteer in the middle. The leader should explain the purpose of the exercise, namely that the group have to stop the volunteer breaking out of the circle without using violence. They must keep arms linked at all times but are otherwise free to move around and bunch together to keep the volunteer contained in the circle. Most people will manage to break out of the circle, but it is a useful precaution to have something like a 90 second limit for each volunteer - this also helps to set a brisk pace for the exercises.

When the person has successfully broken out, or the time limit has expired, a new volunteer can take their place in the centre of the circle. This initial sequence can be repeated several times, or can be alternated with the **first variation**, which involves the volunteer outside the circle trying to break into it.

A **second** variation involves the group facing outwards (still with linked arms) towards the outsider who again has to try and break into the circle.

The leader should ensure that as far as possible all group members have a chance to experience the outsider role. The leader will find a 'neutral' approach useful, which allows space for offers of advice to the group about blocking ploys as well as to the outsider about techniques for breaking through the circle. All variations need not be used in one session. Allow about half an hour for the sequences and up to another half hour for any discussion that is required.

POCOMANIA

Like 'Armadillo', this is a totally silly sequence which is great fun. It can be used with most groups, provided they are in a silly mood! The group should be standing or sitting in a circle, holding hands. The leader nominates someone to start the sequence by making a continuous noise and squeezing the hand of the person on their right who makes a different continuous noise and squeezes the hand of the person on their right who makes another continuous noise, and so on around the circle until everyone is making a noise.

At this point, i.e. when the squeeze returns to the person who started the sequence, they stop making their noise and squeeze the hand of the person on their right who stops making their noise and squeezes the hand of the person on their right, and so on round the circle until silence reigns! The sequence can be repeated several times at different speeds, either clockwise or anti-clockwise. Allow 15 minutes or so.

✳ LINK-UP

A guessing game which can be adapted for use with most groups, large and small.

It is often difficult to anticipate how easy or difficult players will find some of the association cards that have to be made up - it's worthwhile making up two or three sets of cards of increasing difficulty which can be used in one session of the game. This avoids being stuck with one large set of cards which turns out to be far too easy for the group. Use a range of words like: **home; warm; kind; carrot; evil; lovely; money; steal; pain; child,** and make up enough cards to allow each player two or three 'goes'.

The person introducing the game should ensure that people are sitting comfortably in a circle. A volunteer takes the first card and it is explained that they must look at the word on the card and then say out loud any word that it immediately brings to mind. The rest of the group then have the task of trying to guess what the word on the card is. So if someone picks up a card with 'man' on it, they might say 'moustache'. Other people might then guess "face", "hair", "prickly" until someone guesses 'man'. The person who guesses correctly picks up the next card and makes an association, and so on around the group.

Occasionally, people may make rather obscure link-ups which are difficult to guess. In such cases the leader should intervene before players become too frustrated, by asking someone to take another card - perhaps after hearing what the obscure link-up was. With encouragement from adults in the group, the game can be played quite briskly and it usually creates a nice feeling of group achievement. It can be used as a prelude to the 'Word Association Game', and lasts for about 10-15 minutes.

CRISS CROSS NAMING

This game calls for the group to be well acquainted with each other's names. It is suitable for any age group and will work best with large numbers. The game is played with the group standing in a circle. The leader explains that this game has to be played pretty fast and that people will have to concentrate quite hard on what they are doing. A volunteer starts off by calling the name of someone opposite while moving across the circle to take their place. The person named must move off across the circle calling the name of someone else opposite them, before the original person arrives at their place, and so on.

Part of the fun of this kind of game is that it often ends up in confusion! As the leader, you may have to start the group off several times until there is a good rhythm going, which the group will be allowed to continue for several minutes. At this point you can exercise your sadistic tendencies by stopping the game and calling for a rule change which stipulates that two people (and then three) start off the game!

In this kind of sequence, adults should keep tuned in to what the group are getting from it. There is fun to be gained from the confusion and the physical contact when people get tangled up in the middle of the circle, but there can also be considerable shared enjoyment generated by practising the game until it runs (more or less) smoothly. Playing time: 20 minutes. Criss Cross Naming can be played in an initial session after the 'Hello Game' and the 'Ball Game'.

PERSONAL SPACE

This interesting technique is ideal for larger groups. It forces people to recognise the issue of 'personal space', and illustrates in a quite startling way how varied people's personal space boundaries are.

You will find 'Personal Space' is well suited for use before embarking on physical trust games. For example the leader can use the exercise to stimulate discussion on the anxieties we all have from time to time when our own space is invaded inappropriately, or when physical contact becomes an issue. This will provide groups with a good opportunity to discuss the kind of 'groundrules' or 'safeguards' which might be necessary when playing close physical contact games.

The sequence is simplicity itself, and involves splitting your large group into two, with each small group standing with backs to the wall at either end of the room. Choose one small group (group A) to start the sequence and make sure that each person in the group looks down to the other end of the room to identify their 'opposite number'.

Explain that on your signal, group A will walk slowly down to the other end of the room - straight towards their opposite number. Individuals in group B are instructed to raise their hands in front of their chest when they feel that the person from group A has come uncomfortably close to them. The person from group A must immediatly stop dead in their tracks and hold this position.

Once everyone from group A has been stopped by group B putting up their hands, invite people to look around at the different points the A's have been stopped at.

The leader can now lead discussion on the issue of personal space, and some of the factors involved. For example, does the physical size of people make a difference? What about the speed of approach? What about the feelings you have when people get too close? Is this a possible factor in some aggressive/violent incidents?

PASSING THE PERSON

'Passing the Person' is a physical trust sequence best played with a large group. The person introducing the sequence must organise the group into two lines of equal numbers facing each other, and about four feet apart. If it is an odd-numbered group, then the 'odd person out' can be the first volunteer. With even numbers, the leader should ask for a volunteer, and should not participate in the sequence themselves, thus leaving two lines of equal number. As with all physical trust games, adults should be on hand to assist the leader by looking after the safety aspects.

The sequence involves each person crossing arms and holding hands with the person immediately opposite. This forms a chain of hands along which the volunteer can be passed with a rocking motion. They can either take a running jump on to the hands, (not advised for the first time round!), or can be helped by the first two couples at one end lowering their hands so that they can be supported by them and then raised to the same level as the others, before being passed along the line.

Passing the Person can often be played at a cracking pace, as the line of crossed arms provides a very secure support for the person being passed; the difficult bit comes at the end of the pass when the people at the end of the line have to work out how to get the volunteer back on the floor again - simply chucking them off the end of the line is not to be recommended!

An **alternative sequence** can be used which involves the group standing in a tight circle, and passing the person carefully round it. This is a more difficult trust game and demands a lot of co-operation between group members for the person to be passed smoothly round the circle. As with any trust sequence, all players should have a chance to experience it. They are good co-operative experiences for a group and can often be used to round off sessions positively. Allow half an hour or more if both sequences are used.

BACK TO BACK TRUST

This sequence is best suited to small groups, although its spectator element does give it potential for use with larger numbers.

This is a 'Mirror-type' sequence, with similarities to some mime exercises. Two volunteers are required to sit back to back in close physical contact, i.e. with bodies touching from base of the spine to the head. Stools are ideal - chairs with backs impossible - or players can sit on the floor.

The sequence is simplicity itself - Player 1 is asked to move bits of their body in contact with Player 2, e.g. shoulder blades, head etc. Player 2 is instructed to 'mirror' these movements. It often helps if the players keep their eyes shut during the sequence. Allow a few minutes, and then reverse the leadership role, by asking Player 2 to lead off.

Back to Back Trust has a lot of potential, and is undoubtedly capable of variation, e.g. what about all the members of a large group carrying out the exercise simultaneously?

It can also be carried out in groups with pairs standing back to back. This is more difficult for pairs to co-ordinate, and is plenty of fun especially if some humorist decides to bend over!

WHO AM I?

This is a very popular guessing game suitable for small and large groups of most ages. It is based on a well-loved party game. Some equipment is needed, namely a large safety pin, and some sheets of paper with the names of famous personalities or pop stars on them, e.g. 'Madonna', 'Ice-T', 'Wonderwoman', Bruce Forsyth'', etc. The names should be large and clear enough (use a felt marker!) to be easily read at a distance of 6 feet or so. The number of sheets of paper will dictate the length of the game, but allow at least one per player.

The person introducing the game finds someone to go into the middle of the seated circle and explains that that person has to guess the name on the sheet which will shortly be pinned on their back. This is done by them asking questions of other people in the group, who can only answer "yes" or "no". Questions should be asked which will narrow down the range of possibilities, and lead towards a solution.

A series of questions might therefore include ones like this:
"Am I a famous film star?" **"Am I a pop star?"**, **"Am I male?"**, **"Am I alive?"**, **"Do I live in this country?"**, **"Do I live in Australia?"**, **"Am I Kylie Minogue?"**, **"Yes!"**

Asking the 'correct' questions is quite a skill, and some players will require adult help in developing them. This can be done quite simply by having adults take the first few 'goes' therefore offering models for the group to imitate. The game itself can be designed in an **easy version**, if desired, by taking all the famous personalities from one category e.g. pop stars, cartoon characters, footballers.

Adults should help people out by suggesting good questions for them to ask, or areas to explore e.g. age, sex, looks, job, personality etc.

So the game starts with someone in the middle of the circle having a name pinned on their back and turning completely round a couple of times so that the rest of the group can read the name. The person in the middle then has to ask questions of individuals in the group that will help to work out the name pinned on their back. Group members can only answer "Yes" or "No" to questions put to them.

The person can guess the name at any point during the round - if correct, someone takes their place and a new round begins. A time limit, or a limitation as to the number of guesses, can be useful in maintaining pace.

If introduced and explained well, this usually turns out to be a really popular game to play. It builds up social confidence and offers a real sense of achievement as members find they can succeed in guessing 'Who am I?' Playing time: 20-30 minutes or so.

YES/NO

The archetypal 'catch you out' game. Suitable for large and small groups of most ages. YES/NO must be played fairly fast if it is to work properly, so the leader should spend time explaining the rules carefully and organising a 'dry' run.

The leader nominates someone (or obtains a volunteer) who is to be first on the spot, and will answer questions from the rest of the group without saying "yes" (or"aye") or "no". Questions should be fired at this person as quickly as possible, commencing with the person on their right, and carry on right round the group. A time limit, of say, 30 seconds should be imposed for each round. If the person answers "yes" or "no" to any question they are immediately out, and are replaced by the person on the left, and so on round the circle. Anyone completing the 30 seconds should be given a round of applause! The game can be varied and made much more difficult by insisting that replies to questions must be lies!

Allow about 20 minutes' playing time.

CONSEQUENCES

Most folk will have played 'Consequences' at some time in their lives, and it is therefore rare to find a group of young people who can't between them remember the rules of play. 'Consequences' works well in large and small groups and is enjoyed by most ages.

The person introducing the game makes sure that each player has a piece of paper and a pencil. The game involves players writing down a suitable word or phrase for each item in the following list:

1. An adjective applicable to a girl
2. A girl's name
3. An adjective applicable to a boy
4. A boy's name
5. Where they met
6. What she did
7. What he did

8. What she said
9. What he said
10. What the consequence was
11. What the world said.

The sequence works as follows: the leader nominates someone to read out the items from the list, one at a time, making sure that players have enough time to think of, and write down their word or phrase. After each word or phrase has been written down, papers should be folded over so that the writing cannot be seen and passed to the person on the right, before the next item is read out, and so on.

When the sequence has been completed, the papers are read out individually. Players should be asked, when reading, to add in any obvious words needed to maintain continuity.

Consequences is an enjoyable shared experience which invariably produces very funny 'stories'. Often used to round off a session, it takes about 15 - 20 minutes to complete each full sequence.

CLAY MODELLING

A contact game which is useful in introducing the group to mime skills, Clay Modelling involves one person moulding two or three others into an object or situation. There is good spectator value in 'Clay Modelling' and it can therefore be played in large and small groups.

It is suitable for most age groups if care is taken to make the range of objects and situations relevant. These should be worked out in advance of the session and transferred to cards, e.g. 'Two footballers after scoring a goal', 'An armchair', 'A pop star', etc. The cards should also state the number of bodies needed to make each scenario.

The leader should ask for a volunteer who would like to be the first modeller. This person picks a card, but does not tell the group what is written on it. They then choose the number of people stipulated on the card and proceed to mould the people into a sculpture in the middle of the circle.

Many youngsters may need adult help and encouragement to mould the bodies into recognisable objects or situations. The remainder of the group must try to guess what it is. The first person to guess correctly becomes the next modeller, and so on.

With an inexperienced group, the leader may wish to miss out the guessing component, and concentrate instead on encouraging the group to help the modeller by telling them what object or situation the modeller is attempting to create and asking for suggestions as to how this can best be achieved. If each player has a chance to be the modeller, the game can last for 20 minutes + .

LIVING SCULPTURE

This can be a hilarious contact sequence when used in a setting with spectators. But, it also works well in a small group setting. There are similarities with 'Clay modelling', which makes it easy to use the two as a set.

The modelling in this case is done in a fairly random manner, resulting in contortions, chaos and laughter.

The person introducing the sequence requires 7 volunteers, one of whom will be the modeller - this person is required to sit or stand with their back to the others while they form a standing circle and hold hands. The leader should now number off the people in the circle from 1-6 and ask the modeller to shout out action instructions along the lines of: "No. 4 lift up No. l's leg," "No. 3 put your arm round No. 6's neck," "No. 2 crawl through No.4's legs," etc. The group's hands must remain linked for as long as humanly possible, and at some point (preferably prior to the collapse of the group in a heap in the middle of the floor!), the modeller should be instructed to turn round and view the 'Living Sculpture' they have created.

Some 'modellers' may need help in thinking up appropriate instructions and it is important that adult help is offered if it does not come spontaneously from the group. The sequence can be repeated several times and may last for 20-30 minutes.

GUESS THE LEADER

The group should be seated in a circle for this game. It's a very popular guessing sequence which is suitable for young people of most ages and is best played in a large group.

Two volunteers are required to start the sequence off - one to be the 'leader', and another to guess who the leader is. The person who is going to 'guess the leader' should be asked to leave the room, while the group choose a leader whose actions they will all copy. These actions can range from hand-clapping and feet-stamping to the more subtle ones like nose-picking and back-scratching! The leader must regularly change the action and the group must copy immediately.

The action sequence should be started before the volunteer is asked to come back into the room. When they do, they should be asked to stand in the middle of the circle and have three guesses at who the leader is. If they guess correctly, then the leader leaves the room, a new person is selected to lead the group, and the sequence can be repeated. If all three guesses are unsuccessful, the same procedure can be followed.

Most groups pick this game up very easily, provided that the actions are changed regularly by the leader - this gives the person in the middle a fair chance and also helps keep the game moving at a good pace. It can be worth reminding the group not to stare directly at the leader all the time, as this makes it ridiculously easy for the person in the middle. Useful for increasing self-confidence it is a good finisher to the end of a session. Playing time about 20 minutes.

TRUST IN A CIRCLE - THE FEET GAME

This trust sequence is best used as a small group experience with teenagers but it can be used with 8-10 members of a larger group. The games leader should explain the trust concept to the group, taking care to point out the need for everyone to participate for the experience to work properly. The leader should then ask the group to stand in a fairly tight circle, arms outstretched, with a volunteer in the middle.

It is important that the volunteer keeps their arms at their sides, feet together and body rigid. This is no easy matter, but it usually comes after one or two tries and the knowledge that you are not going to land flat on your back! At this stage the volunteer should be asked to relax and enjoy the experience .

The sequence commences with the volunteer leaning backwards until they lose balance; they are then 'caught' by the outstretched arms of the person immediately behind them and pushed gently back towards the centre of the circle.

As trust is built up between the volunteer and the group, they can be allowed to fall further before being caught, and can be pushed to the centre (or around the circle) more energetically.

The leader should take account of the physical size and strength of participants - the sequence will not work with eight average 12 year olds and a 12 stone adult in the middle!

This is particularly important with the more energetic variation: **'The Feet Game'**. This is exactly the same sequence - played sitting down! Players should arrange themselves in a circle on the floor with feet outstretched towards the centre and arms raised to catch the (small!) volunteer in the middle.

Trust sequences like this demand that the adults involved are constantly encouraging feedback between group and volunteer, e.g. "What does it feel like, Jim?", "Is it easier now that you know you're not going to fall?" Adult support and encouragement is crucial in presenting the sequence in such a way that even the most timid youngster will be prepared to 'have a go'. Sequences like these are popular with most groups and are often played two or three at a time to round off an evening's activity. All members of the group should be given the opportunity to experience the sequences. Average playing time for 'Trust': 15-20 minutes.

THE MINISTER'S CAT

Only suitable for small groups, this sequence is useful for increasing the self-image of individuals. The group should be seated in a circle, while the leader explains that the objective is for each person in the group to take it in turns to give the minister's

cat a different adjective, beginning with the same letter, i.e. 'A', 'B', 'C', and so on through the alphabet. The leader can indicate what is required by giving examples of what people might say for the letter 'T', e.g. Bill might say "The minister's cat is a terrible cat", Jean might say "The minister's cat is a tired cat", Irene might say "The minister's cat is a tricky cat", etc.

The sequence starts with the leader nominating someone to give the minister's cat an adjective beginning with the letter 'A'. At the end of each round (i.e. when everyone in the group has given the cat an adjective beginning with the appropriate letter) the person who started the sequence is first to use the next letter in the alphabet. The sequence can be played right through the alphabet, missing out difficult letters like, 'Q', 'V', 'X', 'Y', 'Z', etc, or can be limited to a number of rounds, e.g. 10.

A **variation** exists which requires players to give the cat a name as well as an adjective e.g. "The minister's cat is an ancient cat and its' name is Alfie", "The minister's cat is an amiable cat and its' name is Agnes", etc. Adults in the group should be ready to offer encouragement to players who are having genuine difficulty in thinking of an appropriate adjective or name.

The sequence should not be used competitively - rather as an opportunity for the group to work together to complete the task successfully. 20 mins + playing time, depending on the size of the group.

ADVERB GAME

Adults may have to brush up their miming and acting skills for this game, as it involves acting out various attributes, e.g. acting stupidly, happily, sexily etc. The game always benefits from adults giving a lead, and encouraging withdrawn or embarrassed participants to 'get into it'.

The adverb game is played sitting in a circle, and requires one person to leave the room while an adverb is chosen. The leader can involve the group in choosing an adverb, and should have a few good suggestions in mind, just in case people 'dry up'.

Alternatively, a set of prepared cards can be used, with one being drawn at random each time a new adverb is required.

The player outside the room has the task of guessing which adverb has been chosen - this is done by deduction from the (hopefully accurate!) acting of the other players. They should be reminded that they must answer questions put to them by acting in the manner of the chosen adverb. So, if the adverb is 'aggressive', a player might answer a question like: "What's the time?" by 'squaring up' and saying: "What's it to you?".

When the group is ready, the leader should ask the person outside to come into the centre of the circle and question individual players before trying to guess the adverb. As with similar games, players should be encouraged to use their guesses fairly quickly so that the game has good pace. A new volunteer is required to leave the room (and therefore start off a new round) each time someone runs out of guesses, or manages to name the adverb. This game can be used, with others of similar nature, to promote miming and acting skills. Allow about 15 minutes' playing time.

WOOLLY TALKING

A fascinating groupwork tool which can be used to illustrate which group members' 'hog' the conversation, or rarely contribute etc. Perfect in the small group setting, Woolly Talking might get out of hand in a large group! Players should be seated in a circle and the person introducing the sequence should equip themselves with a large ball of wool! This technique could be used in conjunction with some kind of discussion leader, or simply a 'free for all' conversation.

As soon as someone speaks, the ball of wool should be passed to them, while the leader retains a firm hold on the loose end. The wool is kept taut, and should be passed on to the next person to speak (or attempt to speak!), while the original contributor maintains a secure hold on their bit of wool.

As the conversation progresses, the space in the centre of the circle will soon be taken up with a criss-cross pattern of wool which will show e.g. who spoke the most/least times, who spoke before or after a particular person, etc.

This technique gives tremendous opportunity to the group to analyse several aspects of their verbal interactions.

PYRAMID

'Pyramid' is an exciting physical experience with some of the characteristics of 'Get Knotted!'. Very much a spectator event, the action is performed by five members of a large or small group. The nature of the Pyramid challenge forces the five into close physical contact with each other and necessitates a degree of group co-ordination and planning.

The person introducing the game should ask five volunteers to stand in the middle of the seated circle of 'spectators', and explain that they must arrange themselves so that there are only four feet on the ground. This is the basic challenge, which can be varied to stipulate e.g. two feet and two hands on the ground. A time limit of two minutes or a little longer to complete the task can be used, and it's a good idea to ask the volunteers to hold their Pyramid position for five seconds. If the task isn't completed within the time limit, the volunteers can be given another chance, or can be replaced.

Most kids can work out a solution quite easily, but if they do get into difficulty, adults can encourage the group to offer advice.

There are numerous 'solutions' to Pyramid and this, together with the variables introduced by the physical size of participants, leads to a constantly changing spectator event. Allow 20 minutes' playing time with most age groups.

LIAR

Liar can be used with both small and large groups. It falls into the category of 'silly' games, but it is none the less a useful way of developing mime skills.

The sequence is usually played with the group standing in a circle. The rules are quite simple - you have to mime an activity, and lie about it when your neighbour asks what you're doing!

Someone should be nominated to start the sequence. This person must think of an activity and mime it well enough so that everyone knows what they're meant to be doing (e.g. having a shower). While they are miming their neighbour (on the right, say) must ask "What are you doing?" The first person must lie, so they might say that they're picking their nose, or something like that. The second person must now mime this activity (i.e. picking their nose) and when asked by the person on their right "What are you doing?", they must lie and state that they are doing something completely different, like dribbling a ball. The sequence continues in this way, right round the circle, and can be repeated if required.

It's worthwhile using Liar every now and again, to brush up the group's miming skills. It's a lot of fun to play, and folk usually don't mind being pulled up if their mimes are inadequate. Watch out for overly obscene suggestions and too 'heavy' mime subjects being used to test out participants.

Liar is suitable for most age groups. Allow 10-20 minutes' playing time.

LEVITATION

This trust experience has several variations and it is one of the many sequences where the inter-dependence of group members is illustrated in a practical way. Suitable for all but the youngest groups it can be used as both a small group and 'spectator' experience.

The basic technique is very simple and involves 6 or 8 people offering one another the experience of 'levitation'. As levitation will only be experienced by one person at a time, the leader should stress the need for making this as enjoyable as possible by allowing the chosen person to relax completely. A calm and quiet atmosphere should be suggested.

Once the leader has assembled the 'team', the sequence can begin. The subject should be blindfolded and asked to lie, face upwards, on the floor and relax. It should be stressed to them that the others are going to lift them up and carry them around the room and in no way will they be allowed to fall. The aim of the leader and the team is to reassure the subject and allow them to relax completely and enjoy the experience.

Levitation commences with the team lining up in equal numbers on either side of the subject, squatting down and lifting the person very gently from the floor making sure that the head is well supported and the body is horizontal and straight. The team can now stand and transport the subject at different heights and even above their heads without too much difficulty.

Throughout, the leader should be encouraging feedback from the subject as to how they are feeling, how far they think they are off the ground etc. The scenario created for each subject will differ according to the leader's perception of how well they will handle the sequence.

For example, a timid person may have to be given a lot of positive support throughout, while a more robust youngster might be teased by manufacturing a collision with the 'ceiling'. In reality the ceiling would be something like a plank of wood held by a couple of people just above the subject. If most members of a small group are keen to be levitated, then this sequence can last for 30 minutes or more. Levitation can be used along with other trust games e.g. 'Passing the Person', 'Trust', etc.

I WENT TO MARKET

Sometimes called 'I Went to the Shops', this is a memory game suitable for large and small groups of most ages. The basic idea is that the group builds up a massive shopping list which has to be memorised, added to, and repeated as each player's turn comes round.

The sequence is played sitting in a circle, and begins with a volunteer stating the first item that was bought at the market, e.g.

"I went to market and bought a shirt". Thereafter the sequence continues clockwise with each player adding to the list, e.g. "I went to market and bought a shirt and a tie and a lollipop", and so on round the group.

Players are capable of memorising an amazing number of items, once a few rounds have been played. At this point, the sequence can be started anew, with players being ruled out of the game when their memory fails them.

Allow about 20 minutes+ playing time.

HORROR STORY

Definitely not for the squeamish! This shared experience plays on the adolescent's fascination with the supernatural and other generally horrible things, and demands a fair degree of improvised story telling skill on the part of one of the members of the group.

Horror Story should be introduced quite casually to the group and only carried through if the group are 100% keen on hearing it. The story teller will normally ask something like: "Have any of you heard the story about the wee boy who died in this building years and years ago?" Depending on the response, the story teller will continue. The aim of course, is for the group to drag the story out of him, so initially they might say "I don't really know if I should tell you, 'cos it's a really horrible story!" When at last the group persuade him to continue, he should insist that the lights are switched out so that the room is plunged into total darkness.

The story could centre round the horrible death, 100 years ago, of a boy who had some connection with the building the group are presently using. A plan for such a story might be:

The building used to be a bakery, run by a horrible old man with a foul temper; a boy used to work in the bakery, and quite liked it for a while; but things between him and the baker got steadily worse because of the baker's bad temper. One day they had a terrible argument, and the baker knocked him out and flung him into the deep, damp cellar, where he was left to be eaten alive by rats.

Obviously the success of this experience depends very much on the story teller's ability to improvise and embellish the plot. This is not as difficult as it might seem, bearing in mind that the captive audience are likely to be quite enthralled not to mention terrified by the incredible story.

A quite dastardly **variation** on Horror Story is to include in the plot, the dismembering of a body. At this point, various bits of body can be passed round the group - carrots are good for fingers, peeled grapes for eyes etc.

Allow 20 minutes or so, ideally with a largish group.

THE MINISTRY OF FUNNY WALKS

While we 'oldies' all remember John Cleese and his side-splitting 'funny walk' many young people won't, so it's down to you as games organiser to demonstrate!

Create the Ministry of Funny Walks by first getting the group to divide into two lines, facing each other across the room. The first person in line one walks across to their partner in line two doing a 'funny walk'. The partner in line two then imitates the funny walk as they make their way across to their partner in line one .... and so on until every one has done the funny walk. Don't worry if everyone has fits of the giggles - this is entirely normal in this 'just for fun' sequence.

'The Ministry' now exercises its creative talent for funny walks as you introduce a **variation** which requires the second person to start their go by imitating the first person's funny walk for a few steps only, before inventing their own funny walk .... and so on until everyone has had a chance to copy the previous person's walk and invent one of their own.

Allow 10-15 minutes.

SHOES!

We learned this one the hard way. Yes, it was done to us at a large Youth Participation conference in Hertfordshire. It can be played, if played is the right word, in any size group of six or seven

upwards. The organiser tells everyone in the group, (there were about 100 in our group) to take off their shoes. Once the groans start to disappear, the shoes are taken off. The leader then tells the group to push all the shoes into a pile.

Everyone is asked to step back to the edge of the room and then on the word of command all try and retrieve their own footwear. The resultant free-for-all seems to be good natured and can break down barriers especially at more formal youth events like conferences. Not a game for Doc Marten wearers!

Notes.

Section Three:
PUZZLES AND TWO PLAYER GAMES

The idea of being stuck in the mini bus or car with the chants of
".... why were you born at all ....'' rising in volume gives every
adult who works (or lives) with youngsters the occasional
nightmare. And, as most of us know only too well, it **does**
happen! The situation raises important questions regarding why
we are not equipped with a few ways in which to get the folk in
the transport to enjoy the next half an hour or so, rather than
having to loudly voice their boredom. But then, perhaps we do
have the means to amuse and participate with kids in any situation
where nothing much seems to be going on.

In the section entitled: 'Group Games' we hope that a number of
the games described will have fairly universal applications -
remember, they don't always have to be used as formal class or
group activities. Similarly, in this section we have tried to detail a
range of activities which are often ideal boredom-breakers or time-
fillers. When sensibly used, they will provide a valuable shared
experience and in many cases although the game may be relatively
mundane, you may find yourself the originator of yet another
24-hour wonder!

In this section, the most elaborate equipment you will require for
most of the games and puzzles is paper and pens, a box of
matchsticks, a pack of cards or a pocketful of loose change. We
can almost guarantee that some of the fiendish little puzzles
mentioned in the first part of the chapter will be tried by various
adult users of this book on their unsuspecting, bar-propping
friends. Back in the youth group, we have discovered that an
age-old basic love, which almost all kids share is a good 'trick'.
Hopefully, the ones we offer will fit up a good many sleeves!

LATERAL THINKING

Originally, we believe that this name was coined by Edward De Bono for his own curious brand of side-ways thinking. College common rooms were badly afflicted with the disease in the late nineteen-sixties as devilish situations were dreamed up by the problem setters. The idea is slightly derivative of 'What's My Line?', in that the group or individual can ask questions of the problem setter. The answer they require must be phrased as YES, NO or IRRELEVANT. The winner is the person who first successfully reaches the solution to the original statement. It sounds a bit odd, but it's an extremely easy technique to master and because most of the examples we have listed deal extensively with death and deception, they obviously have immediate appeal to simple child-like minds!

For instance, the problem-setter might say:

"A man is lying dead in the middle of a road with a pack on his back. How did he die?"

Questions might follow this statement, as follows:

Q: Was he run over?
A: No.
Q: Is the road relevant?
A: No.
Q: Is the pack relevant to his death?
A: Yes.
Q: Is it a ruck-sack?
A: No.
Q: Was anyone else involved in killing the man?
A: No.
Q: Did he commit suicide?
A: No.
Q: Did he die accidentally?
A: Yes.
Q: Was his pack too heavy for him?
A: No.
Q: Did he fall from a height?
A: Yes.

Q: Was it a parachute pack?
A: Yes.
Q: And it failed to open?
A: That's right!

The problems are often based around the taken-for-granted way in which the questioners interpret the information they are given. Once they start to enquire more searchingly about the basic original statement, a patch of light may be discovered at the end of the tunnel.

We have included a few problems and their solutions on the next pages. They are only examples and some require a different background of knowledge than others. The group problem solving process can be quite enlightening to the adult(s) involved, especially when one realises that **younger** children very frequently do better at these lateral deductions than the adolescent age range. The time which it takes a group of 3 or 4 youngsters to find the answer they are seeking can vary considerably, but we normally allowed about ten minutes to quarter of an hour for the straight-forward problems and longer for the more convoluted specimens. Be careful that you are sure that all the participants understand the 'words' used well enough to enjoy taking part.

LATERAL THINKING PROBLEMS

1) Q: There is a body floating in a liquid. A woman is annoyed because of this. Why?
   A: There's a fly in the woman's soup.
2) Q: Two dwarves are in a large area, with sawdust and a plank on the ground. One dwarf is smiling, the other is dead. Why did the dwarf die?
   A: It would appear that the first dwarf had grown. The circus dwarf measured herself against the plank, thought that she was growing and committed suicide.
3) Q: A man with a towel around his waist is standing next to a horse. What is he doing?
   A: There are at least two possible answers. (1) He is letting his clothes dry out on a clothes horse, OR (2) he has just finished a gym session on the vaulting horse.
4) Q: There is a girl hanging by a rope from the ceiling, with her

toes two feet above the ground. She is dead. In the corner of the room, out of reach, is a bucket and in the middle of the room, underneath the feet of the girl is a pool of water. How did she die?

A: She froze a bucket of water, turned the bucket upside down, and let it slightly melt. She then put the bucket in the corner of the room and stood on the melting ice with the rope around her neck.

5) Q: Anthony and Cleopatra are lying on the floor. Around them is broken glass and water. What has happened?

A: Anthony and Cleopatra are goldfish, their goldfish bowl has been broken.

6) Q: Every day a man returns home to his flat, gets in the lift and goes up to the 7th floor, gets out and walks up another 3 floors to his flat. Why?

A: He's a dwarf and he cannot reach higher than the 7th button for the lift.

7) Q: A woman goes into a bar and asks for a drink and the barman shoots off a gun into the air. The customer says "thanks". Why?

A: She had hiccups and the bang made them go away!

8) Q: There is a man who goes to a Doctor's surgery and asks to have his arm amputated. Why?

A: Three men were shipwrecked in a small rowing boat with no food. One man was a surgeon and he was chosen to amputate one arm from each person to use as food. When it came to his turn they had reached an island, but since they had agreed that **each** provide an arm, the surgeon had to have his arm cut off on his return to civilisation.

PUZZLES & GAMES

Frustrating your neighbour, colleague or best friend is a pretty popular pastime. Doing this using the medium of paper and pencil, matchsticks, coins and playing card puzzles etc. has a certain enjoyment value which can be devoid of spitefulness, since it is distinctly possible that the person who is on the receiving end the first time round will very soon be the protagonist.

On a slightly evil note, think how clever all the youngsters you know are going to think you are when you start plying them with these problems!. More seriously, you may be pleasantly surprised how well these can work with introverted youngsters, who don't much like getting involved with the group, but who, nonetheless, are highly delighted with the opportunity to pit their wits against you at a quite intimate level.

MATCHBOX LIFT

This requires a little bit of practice, but once that has taken place it is quite addictive. The idea is to lift up one matchbox onto another one (which is on end) keeping the central finger firmly on the table at all times. The matchbox which is to be lifted must be gripped between the 2nd and 4th fingers.

Keep the matchbox to be lifted close to the one which is going to serve as a pedestal. Keep the pressure firmly on the central finger. Angle the two fingers used for gripping so that the front of the

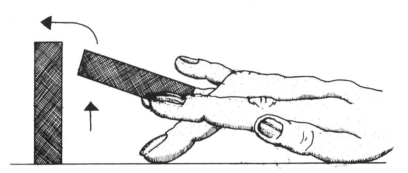

matchbox is tilted upwards and therefore is more likely to make it to the top.

Three tips:

a) Keep the matchbox to be lifted close to the one which is going to serve as a pedestal.
b) Maintain the pressure firmly on the central finger.
c) Angle the two fingers used for gripping so that the front of the matchbox is tilted upwards and therefore is more likely to make it to the top.

With even more practice you can do this with a matchbox and a king-size pack of cigarettes!

MATCHBOXES

This one is a brain teaser although once the answer is known it appears stupidly simple.

The challenge is to place six matchboxes in a combination so that each one touches every other one.

The solution we know is this:

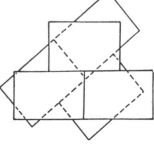

TRIANGLES

We're sure that you've been annoyed by this sort of puzzle before!

The aim is to move only 3 matches to make 3 absolutely new triangles.

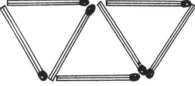

The solution is rather in the order of the Lateral Thinking Problems. You can pick up any three matches and reach the answer as below. As you can see, you must be thinking three-dimensionally.

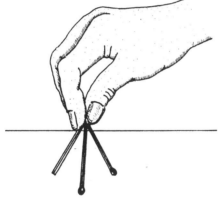

BALANCING COINS

The answer to this one makes use of a bridge-building principle, but don't tell your willing participants that before they start!

The aim is to place a pile of at least nine 2 pences on top of a £5 or £10 note (or a £1 note if you're a Scottish reader!) at a central point (x in the diagram) across the top of the mug. The contestant may not hold the note while trying to balance the coins, nor may other items be used to hold the note in place.

To perform the amazing feat, the balancer must be provided with a fairly new bank note. The solution requires corrugating the note to provide a sturdy platform for the coins:

THREE KNIVES

This is 'borrowed' from De Bono. Apologies. It's a great item if you can provide enough milk bottles, knives and glases and don't have anyone in your group who knows the solution.

For each contestant or group you need 3 knives, three milk bottles and a glass - for safety and financial reasons, probably unbreakable. The aim is to balance the glass on the knives which in turn are on the bottles. The tops of the bottles are just a little more than knife's distance apart and form a triangle.

The answer is cunning and involves an appreciation of weaving. Based on the same principle as closing up the flaps on a cardboard box, the knives are knitted together, so they provide a firm platform. In this shape they can be rested across the tops of the 3 bottles and easily support a carefully placed glass.

The knives are linked like this:

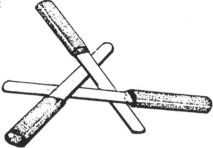

FOUR STRAIGHT LINES

The problem is to draw a continuous line comprised of four straight line sections, to connect every dot together. These straight lines may cross each other, but not double back i.e. ⋈ is O.K.; ⟋⟍ is incorrect

The answer is pure lateralism:

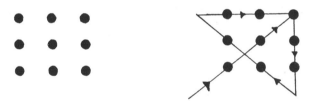

SIX STRAIGHT LINES

As an alternative to the 4 straight lines puzzle, try offering this challenge to your young friends!

The aim is to join up all sixteen dots with only six lines, You must not go over the same line twice, nor take the pen off the paper.

And the answer is:

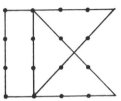

NUMBER 6

This can misfire if the kids you try it with don't have a basic knowledge of numbers, but in most groups it has resulted in a fair laugh for all. Ask the participants to move two out of the 3 matches to make 6. The wording is intentionally ambiguous. So is the answer:

THE STAR

A quickie! Snap 4 matches, but don't pull them apart. Gently bend the broken matches, so that the joint bends freely. Then place them on a smooth topped table (not mother's best) in the following shape:

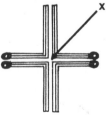

Tell your onlookers that they must rearrange these matches into a star shape WITHOUT touching them.

The answer is to pour a small quantity of liquid into the centre 'X' of the matches. To achieve the required result, the liquid must be very carefully applied at this intersection. We use another match to drip the liquid into the intersection. Then, sit back and the matches will behave as an automaton. It may take a couple of minutes to work, so be patient.

BLACK MAGIC
Appealing to younger children, this is a cunning little oddity which requires two accomplices who are supposedly in telepathic contact with one another. What happens is that one of the team goes out of the room while the other stays with the audience, who are invited to choose an object for the outside telepath to recognise. Once the object has been chosen, the person outside the room returns and the 'telepath' who knows what the object is starts asking their accomplice, "Is the object this ....?". Each time the answer is "No", until there is a black coloured object mentioned. Then, the **next item** indicated will be the one which was agreed upon at the outset.

Everyone realises that they are being tricked, but how it is done can keep the group guessing for some time. The accomplice in the room must, to maintain the secret, vary the 'black' objects around, otherwise the way in which the subterfuge has been perpetrated is rather obvious.

ELEVEN AND SIXTEEN
Mathematicians can feel free to write in and explain to us how this one works. Whatever the mechanics, it is a fine trick and comes courtesy of Colin, a part-time Lothian Youth leader.

To commence the action you say that you are going to randomly deal out the pack into piles across a table top. Make sure that you don't try to copy us too perfectly - we were left wondering why the trick wouldn't work for nearly quarter of an hour before realising that the pack was not numbering fifty-two! When you deal out the cards, face up, you in fact are making piles which add up to 11, based on the first card dealt. So, if you place down a 4 **you then add another 7 cards**; if it is as an Ace, **add 10 cards**; with a Jack or King etc, you would add only **1 card**.

Do this until the pack looks as though it is running out and then make a comment, such as:
"That should be enough piles for you to choose from."

At which point you separate the discards and leave them to one side. Then turn over all the piles, so they are face down.

Ask the 'client' to choose 3 piles while you have your eyes closed. They must look at the top card from each of the 3 piles and total up the score value which they have without telling you the score. The piles can be moved from their present position, it makes no difference. You then pick up all the cards in the other piles including discards and deal them out in piles across the table. Appear to be putting them in different size piles for some reason, while in fact you are counting up to 16. Once you reach 16, re-start the counting and the number of cards you are left with is the TOTAL SCORE count of the 3 cards at the top of the 3 face down piles.

DAVID LOVEL

This effort is brought to you by Christine Brotherston, an East Lothian youth club member - we thought that it was fascinating and unusual.

First: Ask your victim to shuffle a pack of cards. Then deal out ten pairs of cards, face downwards.

Secondly: Request that a card be taken from the top of two of the pairs. These should be memorised and then replaced as a **New Pair,** the remaining two cards also being replaced as a pair. (This process takes place while the magician, or whatever, turns away.)

Thirdly: All the cards are picked up and the pile is then dealt out following the memorised dealing system, as follows. The first card is placed at 'D' in DAVID; the second goes to the other 'D' position at the end of DAVID. The third card is put at 'A' in 'DAVID' and the fourth goes to the other 'A' which is in ABBEY. This dealing sequence continues until all the cards have been placed into the 5 x 4 distribution. The last cards to be placed will be the two 'Bs' in ABBEY.

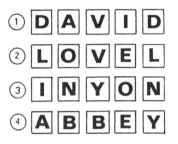

Finally: Once all the cards are positioned, ask the assistant to state which row or rows their original pair of cards are now in. Armed with this information, as long as you can remember the mnemonic, you can immediately spot the two cards by finding the only two letters which appear either in the one or two rows indicated. It's so devious that the result is highly impressive and no-one will ever guess how the trick is done.

ONE IN THE MIDDLE

A well known card trick can still be one of the best. Taking a pile of cards which is a multiple of three, say 21, deal the cards into 3 piles face upwards and while this is being completed, ask a friend to memorise a card. At the end of the distribution, the 'client' indicates which pile, out of the 3, the chosen card is in. You then casually pick up the 3 piles, but be very careful that the chosen pile is placed in the **middle**. Repeat this process twice more, after which you deal out the cards from the pack (which is face down). Stop at the card which is the higher side of the midway point i.e. with 21 cards the hidden card is 11. When 'finding' the card at the end of the sequence it is best to appear to be scrutinising each card carefully, before finally making the selection.

ISLANDS

We were told about this one and managed to make a mistake in the rules when we first learned it. But then, Michael, the originator of the trick met us just before the manuscript had to go to the binders, and here we are again! You have to tell the audience a little story. Take the 4 top value cards of each suit A, K, Q, & J and deal them into their respective suits, laid out so that the value of each card is showing. Once this is done, tell the audience that each suit represents a tribe who live on a different island.

Up until now there has been no contact between the tribes. Then you put the 4 piles together one suit on top of the next and say that there has been a war and the tribes get rather mixed up! Shuffle the pile in the following manner; taking any number of cards from the top of the pile, place them besides the main pile, place the rest of the main pile on top of them. You can repeat these sequences as often as you like and invite the audience to join in. Say to them that something amazing has happened. All the islanders have decided to live in peace. Then deal out the cards into 4 piles, 1st card in each pile first, then 2nd etc. The result is a complete mix, 4 different suits/tribes, each with the same balance of Ace, King, Queen and Jack represented in each pile.

WHICH PICTURE CARD?

Budding graphic artists and students of antique games paraphernalia will no doubt have noticed that the printing on old playing cards and the like tends to be eccentric. A card trick can be based on the misalignment of printing on the court or picture

check the
width of
this margin

cards in an old pack. It's rather reminiscent of 'find the lady', but performed face upwards. Place three or four court cards in a row; it doesn't matter what values you use. With you not looking, challenge the audience to move any card round e.g. the Jack.

Obviously, with playing cards there is no difference between one end and another, or is there? When you, as the card-master, turn round, you carefully scrutinise the cards. What the audience do not realise is that there is a minute difference in margin width between one end of each card and the other, so, in turning one card around the movement can be recognised. When originally setting out the cards, you must be careful to put all the cards around the same way, i.e. with the large or small width margin at the top.

COIN PUZZLES

There are a large number of these in existence, many of which are of the "in the fewest possible moves .... variety." We do not intend to duplicate the books which cover this subject, but we include some examples so that you are aware of the style. Perhaps you could invent a few new ones of your own!

CHANGEOVER

With the following formation, move only 3 coins to reverse the triangle so it points down rather than up. It might even win you a coke!

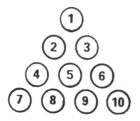

The answer is: Move 7 to the left of 2; 10 to the right of 3 and 1 to the bottom of 8 and 9.

Easy when you know how!

ROLL OVER

This is a 'once only' guessing game.

Place two coins A & B together and ask your audience, which way up the A coin will be if the A coin is rolled around the B coin. Will it be upside down;upright or sidewise on when it reaches the other side? To do it easily, try it on a carpet or similar.
Try it and find out the answer!

COIN FOOTBALL

Ever since we gave up classroom darts games, using rather decrepit compasses and other more unmentionable pursuits, we thought that we had forgotten completely about coin football. A couple of recent journeys with the kids on the renowned 'earth-shrinking 125' from Edinburgh to London have changed all that!

So, on to coin football. The rules are as varied as any other traditional game. The pitch is any smooth table top. Usually a number of large coins (say 3 x 2ps for each team) are used as players, heads for one team, tails for the other. Then, the ball is a 1 p. The players may be propelled with a flick of the finger as in Subbuteo or with a short plastic or wooden ruler. The latter method, if rulers are available, makes the game fairer.

The duration of the game is decided and sides are chosen. 5 minutes each half is probably long enough. Players are positioned by hand before a kick off, then with no opposing players within 3" of the ball, the 'player' taking kick-off is shoved on to the ball which is kicked up the field.

One kick per turn is the rule, unless:
1) The ball is kicked into another player on the same team.
2) A free-kick has been awarded.

Fouls are given for:
1) Touching the ball with the ruler hand.
2) Touching an opposition player with the ruler hand.
3) Hitting an opposition player with a player **before** striking the ball.
4) Moving a player by hand, except where allowed for in the rules.

At free-kicks, any players may be re-positioned by hand, but opposition players must be at least 3" away from the ball.

Throw-Ins become in this game, 'kick-ons'. This happens if the ball goes out of play over the side lines. Corner kicks and goal kicks are taken as in real football and constitute an opportunity to re-position players, and the 3" rule applies.

After a goal it is a kick off from the centre mark.

We found that as a journey-shrinker this game did us more good than British Rail!

KERCHECK

A 2 player game which we found popular with a mixture of I.T., Youth Training and Youth Club kids. Use a normal draught board or rule out your own board on a piece of card, and lay out 1p's and 2p's as indicated.

The **rules** are:
1) Coins can move one square, horizontally, vertically or diagonally.

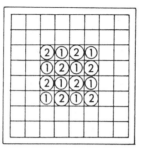

2) Moving **away** from an opposing coin means that it is captured.

3) You may only move if you can move away from an opposing coin.

4) The game ends when neither player makes a capture.

5) The player with most pieces left wins.

Since the rules are a reversal of those used in most games it adds to the interest value.

REVERSI

This is the two player game upon which the commercial 'Othello' mentioned elsewhere in this book is based. An 8 x 8 or 10 x 10 board can be used and the game is played using coins. 'Heads' and 'tails' determine ownership and the idea is to cover the board with more of your pieces. The Summer Scheme at Canongate in Edinburgh was 'Proving Place' for this game and it was a successful alternative to its more expensive counterpart.

You'll need 64 coins for the 8x8 board. One player is heads, the other tails.

The idea is to sandwich your opponent's pieces. You can place a coin with either head or tail showing, anywhere where it will enclose any number of the opponent's coins. This placement may be diagonal, vertical or horizontal as long as it is in a straight line.

You may only go if you can make a sandwich and when you do this you turn over all the coins between your two coins. It is quite possible to make more than one line at a time. It is equally and annoyingly likely that you will sometimes make sandwiches which will benefit your competitor more than you. If you can make a sandwich you must go. Play continues until all the spaces are filled. You then count up who has the most coins - heads or tails. See Othello (Commercial Games) for more comments.

SQUARE OF FIVE

With coins set out as below, rearrange them so that they are in a square where you can count 5 along each side.

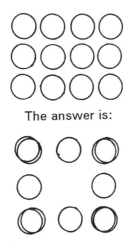

The answer is:

FOX AND GEESE

One of the traditional games, this can also be played with coins, buttons or tiddly-winks. One player moves the Fox, the other moves the Geese.

The fox is represented by the one counter in the centre of the board and the geese are 13 in number and positioned as above. All pieces may move one point along an unobstructed line. The fox must try to jump over geese to a vacant spot beyond, which knocks that goose off the board. He may jump more than one goose per turn, as long as there is a vacant point on which to land. The player who is moving the geese must try to block the fox in, so that he cannot move. The fox aims to 'eat' so many geese that there are no longer enough to block him in.

The board is:

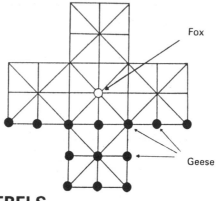

Fox

Geese

CHINESE REBELS

Very much in the fox and geese family of two player games this is useful as a simple diversion with all age groups. The board is simple to draw on a large piece of paper and 20 counters or coins of one sort are needed, and one of a different type.

The general and the rebels all move one circle forwards, backwards or sideways, but the general can also 'kill' rebels by hopping over them, at which point they are removed from the board. No piece may move diagonally.

The general aims to either reach camp or to kill enough rebels to make himself safe. The rebels try to surround the general or corner him, so that he can't move.

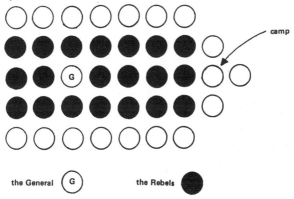

the General (G)   the Rebels ●

Not a bad game, though not one which is likely to become a regular favourite. Certainly it is a useful addition to the repertoire.

GOMUKU

This is a large scale noughts and crosses. It is an alternative which is popular with younger groups. A photocopied board/sheet of paper is quite a good idea if your employer is feeling benevolent! Draw up a board with 19 horizontal lines.

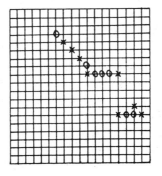

After this, players take turns to draw noughts and crosses on the intersections. Five in a line wins.

PIT OR MU-TORTURE

This is said to be a Maori game, but as it is simple and two players can play it on any improvised board, whatever the size, it is thoroughly suitable for the purpose of playing with young people.

The aim is to make it impossible for your opponent to go. Start with 4 pieces each (of different colours) on adjacent points of the star shape. (only one piece at a time is allowed in the Pit).

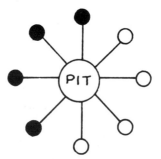

A piece may be moved on to a next adjacent star point OR into the PIT, or out of the pit onto another star point. A piece can only be moved into the PIT when one or both of the adjacent star points are occupied by an opponent's piece.

Play ceases when one player cannot move. The game is more intricate and lasts longer than you might expect.

NINE MEN'S MORRIS

Draw up a board, as in the diagram, then with nine coins each (heads and tails), this game is easily improvised. Each player puts one coin in turn on an empty point (an intersection between two lines) on the board. The aim is to make a line of 3, at which point that player may remove an opponent's coin. (This should be a coin which is not in a line of 3 unless there is no other coin available.) Once all the counters have been played, players move one of their pieces to a neighbouring point. They still try to make rows of 3

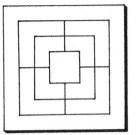

and rows can be broken and remade with the same diminishing effect on the opponent's force. Blocking an opponent so that they cannot move, or reducing the opponent to less than 3 coins ends the game.

ROMAN DRAUGHTS

They don't come much simpler than this! For 2 players. Jumping over opponent's pieces removes them from the board. As with draughts, reaching the backline allows players to move forwards or backwards. A move is one square or a hop. The aim is to remove all the opposing pieces, or to force a draw.

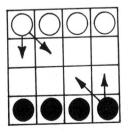

THE FOOTBALL TEAM

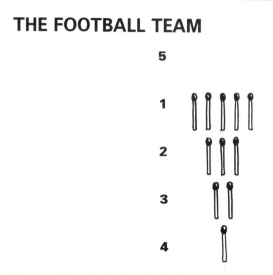

Matchsticks do look a little like men, and in the above formation they represent the old-fashioned 'line-up' of a football team. Ask your kids to re-arrange them moving only 4 matches, so that the entire team is facing in the opposite direction. The answer involves moving a single match in ROW 4 to ROW 5 and then 3 matches move from ROW 1 to ROW 3 and that's it.

NIM

The same formation can be used for a two player game. Choose who goes first, then that player may remove any number of matches from a line, including the whole line. The other player does the same and the aim is **to leave the opponent with the last match**. The game is quite annoying, but popular with a wide age range, since it is so easy to play even if making sure you win is more of a problem.

KAYLES

Another matchstick game for two. Between 20 and 30 matches are normally used. The matches are placed in a long row end to end and on each turn one match can be removed, or two if they are touching. These are the only rules. Unlike in the game of NIM, the winner is the person who picks up the last match.

MAXEY

This is a good game. There, we have committed ourselves!! Seven parallel lines should be drawn on a piece of paper, each should be roughly the length of a match and they should be slightly less than

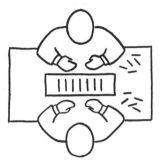

a match-length apart. Each player has 5 matches and the paper should be placed so that the lines point towards each player. One match is played at a time and they are placed along the lines with the match heads pointing towards the player. If two matches are side by side, then a player may opt to play a match resting across the two. This is done with the match head pointing to the right.

Scoring is as follows:
1 point for each match played adjacent to another match.
2 points for each match played across adjacent matches.

The highest scoring player is the winner.

GALE

David Gale, associate Professor in Maths at Brown University in the States invented this little diversion. It is a game of strategy and involves 2 players using different coloured pens or pencils. In the diagram the solid dots represent those belonging to Player A and the small circle dots are those for Player B. The direction of play for each player is also shown on the diagram. Taking alternate turns, each player joins any 2 of his or her dots together with a single line. This can only be done in either a horizontal or vertical direction. Whilst Player A is trying to join the bottom and top sides of the grid together, Player B is trying to join up the left and right sides.

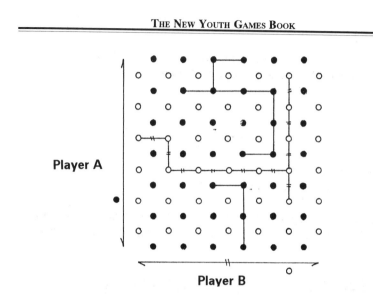

Player A

Player B

The winner is the first player to make a continuous line joining their 2 sides together. No lines may cross.

This is an ideal alternative game to the well known 'boxes' syndrome. With 'Sprouts' described next, they form quick paper and pencil games which will be new to most young people.

SPROUTS

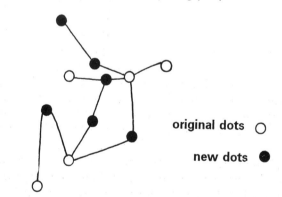

original dots ◯

new dots ●

Originating from Cambridge, this has proved a successful paper and pencil game in almost all settings with a wide range of age groups.

To start with, about 5 or 6 dots are drawn on a piece of paper. Taking alternate turns, 2 players draw a line either joining two dots or joining a dot to itself. They then draw a new dot in anywhere along the line they have just made.

There are 3 rules:

1) No line may cross itself, or cross a line that has already been made.
2) No line may be drawn through a dot.
3) A dot may only have 3 lines leaving it.

The last person who can successfully draw a legitimate line is the winner. The game is more fun than 'boxes' and nowhere near as widely known.

CROSSWORDS

A	B	O	U	T	6
B	R	A	G	X	4
O	I	R	R	R	O
P	Q	P	A	O	O
C	A	R	T	M	4
O	O	3	3	O	

This is a painless form of word game which can be played by two players or more. Each player needs to draw a square 5 x 5 to fill in, or use previously photocopied squares. Players in turn call out a letter and everyone, including that player must write that letter in a square. Players must be careful to keep their own squares hidden from each other. Play continues until all the boxes are filled.

The aim is to make words either horizontally or vertically. The shortest word which counts is 2 letters in length, the longest, obviously 5 letters. Each letter scores 1 point for a player when it is part of a word. A five letter word scores 5 plus 1 bonus. You may score more than one word in a line but they must not be touching; so it would have to be two, two-letter words with another letter in between. Be sensitive when using this game if there are young people who are poor at spelling and might feel threatened by being shown up.

GET OUT OF JAIL!

This is a fiendish puzzle which normally has participants frustrated and stuck in jail! To enable people to have a few goes at the puzzle it is best to photocopy a few of the jail drawings.

What you tell people is that they must try to get from their cell marked with a cross and out of the exit via **all the other cells**, by going in and out of each other cell only once. It is not easy!

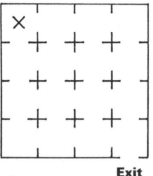

And the solution is:

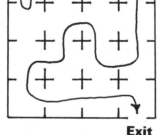

Exit

CULTURAL GAMES

MORA/SCISSORS, PAPER, STONE

Kids around the world will teach these games to adults if they are interested. It is surprising how quickly we unlearn our heritage.

Mora is a game of fingers. It is usually played by 2 players holding closed fists against their chests, while facing one another. At a given signal they 'throw' a number of fingers; a closed fist indicates '0'. Simultaneously, they both shout a total for the two players' 'throws of fingers.' A cry of 'Mora' indicates ten. After fifteen rounds, or so, a clear winner should emerge, and hopefully a slice of noisy fun.

We have found that playing this with kids gave rise to disputes; but even with us acting as referees didn't wholly avoid the problem. Let us know if you find the answer. (The game can be played calling odds or evens and one or two hands can be used. Obviously a draw is very likely in this variation.)

Scissors, paper, stone can start the same way as Mora, or the hands can be held behind the back. At an agreed signal, both players display their hand either as a clenched fist (stone); fingers in a V (scissors) or as an open palm (paper). The pecking order for the hands is as follows:

PAPER ENCLOSES STONE
STONE BLUNTS SCISSORS
SCISSORS CUT PAPER
TWO SYMBOLS THE SAME IS A DRAW

SPOOF

Like so many other games which we have enjoyed playing with kids this one started life in pubs (we think). There's nothing much simpler, yet it is a game which is not as commonly known as we expected.

Here goes .... Ask everyone (from 2 to lots of players) to take out 3 coins and explain to them that they must each place between 0 and 3 coins in a closed fist and place it on the table in front of them. This process is completed out of sight of the other players. Once all the players have put their mits on the table they each have a guess at the TOTAL NUMBER OF COINS in all the hands. No two people may choose the same number. Once everyone has made a guess, everyone shows their coin count.

If someone guesses the correct number, they drop out and play continues with new selections of coins being made. If no-one makes a correct guess, everyone re-selects a new handful of coins or sweet nothingness. The person having first 'guess' circulates around the group.

The final loser is the person left 'in,' who has not found the correct number at any point during the game. With 2 players, it is best to play a best of 3 sequence. The loser in a pub will normally buy a pint; we played the game with kids' groups using forfeits. Six foot three adults crawling around the floor on their knees in a public coffee-bar muttering "Why was I born so small?" to the customers, seemed to amuse our teenagers. We can't understand why!

KNUCKLY

Most people should remember this two player game. It involves players taking turns at rapping each other's knuckles with their clenched fist. Play commences with the players facing each other, either standing or seated. The forearm should be outstretched with fist clenched and the back of the hand uppermost. The two players then move their fists together until the top joints of the fingers are touching.

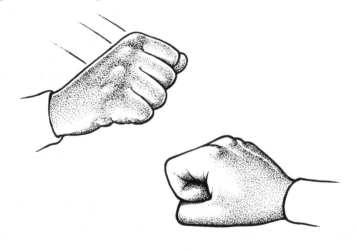

One person is nominated to start, and tries to rap the other person's knuckles before they can be withdrawn. If they succeed they continue to get another shot until they miss, at which point play passes to their opponent, and so on. An enjoyable but sometimes painful way of spending 10 minutes!

For those less masochistic, however, an alternative method is to use open palms instead of clenched fists i.e., players move their finger **tips** together as opposed to joints and hence they would receive a slap from an open palm, much kinder than a rap from a clenched fist!

PITCH AND TOSS

One of the very regional games much associated with either being young or gambling, depending upon from where you have come.

It's an alternative, or derivation of the simple heads or tails coin-toss. In the form we describe it we believe it to be a Scottish pastime, though it probably evolved during the First World War. Once taught to kids it can spread back into the classroom world, so you may be given reason to look furtive when the new source of debate reaches the staffroom or the P.T.A. meeting!

A piece of wood is stuck in the ground, or a bottle is laid on the floor about 10 yards away. Coins are thrown (pitched) and the person who has thrown the nearest coin to the target is allowed to pick up all the coins, place them along the forearm and then toss them from this place into the air. All the coins landing on the ground as heads are then traditionally regarded as the pitch and tosser's property. Those left over were used for another toss, by the 2nd closest pitcher until all are accounted for.

LEG WRESTLING

This competitive 2 player sequence is a test of strength and technique and operates well as a spectator event.

Two volunteers are required to lie on the floor, side by side, in the centre of the circle. They should be lying in opposite directions to each other player. The two legs are then crooked round each other at the back of the knee joint, and battle commences!

The aim is simply to exert sufficient leg pressure sideways to throw your opponent off balance and force their leg over onto the ground. There is a marked similarity to arm wrestling - but it's much more fun with legs.........honest!

CHINESE WRESTLING

We got quite a shock when the best player of this game in a mixed youth group turned out to be a twelve year old young lady called Trudi!

Anyway, on to the game. It's a good alternative to 'Leg Wrestling' and just as fun. Two people stand close together with their backs touching. They then reach down with their hands through their legs and clasp hands with the other person. The aim is to try and pull the other person over a line on the floor. Winning is as much about technique as about strength.

APPLE CUT

This is another devious little trick, especially popular with younger children. As the presenter, you suggest that someone might like to try their hand at cutting the peel off an apple in one continuous spiral. Prior to the exercise, you have been doctoring the apple or apples to be used. What you have done is cut the apple into **segments from the inside** of the peel.

Puzzled and confused? Well, the answer is somewhat unexpected: take a long, thin needle and a piece of strong cotton and thread the needle in and out of the apple as shown in the diagram. Keep hold of the trailing end and then when the needle has circumnavigated the apple back to the point of entry at 'X', pull both pieces of cotton through the apple, using the cotton in the same way as a cheese is dissected with a length of wire.

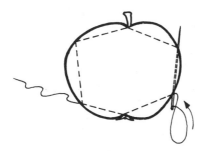

The procedure can be repeated with a horizontal version across the apple - this leaves the apple in quarters. If you are careful, the result is not really detectable and extremely odd. It can also be used to dissect a banana into lots of sections....

MOTOR CAR/MINI-BUS GAMES

DRIVING BLIND

The driver silently chooses an object in the distance and tells all the passengers to close their eyes (not the driver's, NOTE !). Each passenger can then open their eyes whenever they like and call out 'NOW'. The player who is nearest in distance and time to the driver's object is the winner and scores a point. A complete game can be up to any number of points as agreed beforehand.

GUESS THE DISTANCE

We didn't invent this one, but it's quite an obvious game for journeys. An object in the distance is chosen and each occupant guesses the distance from a given moment in time. The most accurate guess, based on the milometer reading is the winner. We hope that your local authority bus has a dial that works!

PUB SIGNS

This is based on having good eyesight and some imagination. All the occupants of the vehicle look out for pubs and win a point if they are the first to correctly name the pub. Signs are often misleading, so it often takes 3 or 4 guesses from different passengers to get it right. Score one point per correct sign. Any advance on the 'Shoulder of Mutton and Cucumber'?

SUMS

Passengers take turns to 'adopt' a car registration number as it is passed by or passes the car or mini-bus. Say for instance John's car has a registration XYZ249, they score $2+4+9=15$. The aim of the game is to be the first player to obtain an EXACT score of **50**; 51, or 52 etc. won't count and going over takes a player back to zero. An endless sort of affair, it can be played anywhere there are other vehicles, which gives it an advantage over 'Pub Signs' in the more remote country regions.

A second version can be played if you have paper and pencils for each player. Again each player adopts a number plate of successive passing cars, but this time the number element is written down as a number with units, tens and hundreds i.e. GMK 192 becomes 192. On the next car or van or whatever, that the player adopts, 192 is added to the new number, say 940; i.e.

$$192 + 940 = 1132$$

This process is continued up to a limit. We suggest 50,000, which if it works, keeps a whole mini-bus occupied throughout a trip. The first contestant with a score over 50,000 wins.

Notes.

Notes.

Section Four:
THE HEAVY END

(See the Relationship Games Introduction on page 13, as a refresher on 'how to use' this type of sequence, before using games from this section).

PICTURE YOURSELF

This is an excellent exercise which is well suited to the 'beginning' stages of a new group. For maximum learning for group members, 'Picture Yourself' should be repeated towards the middle of the group's life, and again at the end. Used in this way, the technique can offer insights into growth and development which has taken place - as seen by the individuals themselves.

'Picture Yourself' helps young people to learn about themselves. As the technique relies on (basic) drawing skills rather than verbal ability, some quite subtle insights can be gained which would never come out using a verbal technique alone. The exercise is invaluable in 'therapeutic type' groups and can furnish the adult leader with significant insights about individuals around the areas of confidence, self-esteem, interests, important issues etc.

'Picture Yourself' is very easy to organise; all you need are sheets of flipchart paper (or similar) and a good supply of coloured markers. Make sure that each person has access to as many different coloured pens as they need - colour is a very important feature of most people's pictures. Allow individuals 20 minutes to draw a picture of themselves. This picture should represent the important things about the individual, their lifestyle, aspirations etc. Make it clear to the group that each person will be expected to introduce themselves to the group by talking to their own completed picture.

The leader's main tasks are to help individuals complete their pictures (e.g. if they get 'stuck') and to ensure that they are clearly explained. Ask questions, encourage the group members to help each other, as each person introduces their picture 'in the round'. The leader may want to debrief the session by highlighting some of the similarities and differences between the pictures. Are there any common aspirations or fears, for example? Issues identified may be suitable for the group to work on at a future date through discussion or in another relationship game etc.

This flexible technique helps you to assess where members of your group are coming from. When repeated later on with a group, 'Picture Yourself' demonstrates growth and personal achievement. The technique underlines that your 'picture' never stays the same and is influenced by life experiences and events.

The total time needed for this game depends on the size of the group - as each person must describe what is in their own picture. With a group of eight the sequence might take up the best part of an hour - we don't recommend that it should be used with groups much larger than this.

CARD INTRODUCTIONS

This is a very useful introduction game and can be used with people who are meeting for the first time. First, cut out cards which are about post card size - one for each member in the group. Believe it or not, that's all the preparation you have to do for this sequence - just make sure that you have enough pens for each group member.

With a group of between 6 and about 15 invite each member to write the numbers 1 to 5 down the left hand side of their cards:

```
1.
2.
3.
4.
5.
```

The leader then tells the participants to write various 'answers' against each of the numbers. The 'questions' are your own choice; they resemble the old-style Pop Star Questionnaires. Against number 1, you might ask everyone to write 'the name they want to be known as in the group'; against number 2, the person they admire most (living or dead)'; number 3, 'favourite food'; number 4, 'the behaviour that annoys them most'; and, number 5, 'if you weren't here, where would you prefer to be'.

It can be used as a basic introductory session, but it's not a good idea to use it with too young a group. When everyone has filled in their cards, invite them all to pass their cards to the person on their left. Then, each person introduces, in turn, the person to their right, to the rest of the group. Depending on the questions you have chosen to ask you can encourage the sharing of information (e.g. favourite person) which would not normally 'come out' during a first meeting. This sequence also works well as an icebreaker in staff training sessions where people are meeting together for the first time. Allow about 10-15 minutes.

GROUP MIME GAME

This works well as a spectator event within a large group, but it can easily be used with smaller ones. Mime cards need to be prepared in advance and these can be designed to cater for the group's interests, allowing the Mime Game to be used with diverse groups and ages. Some examples of Mime cards are as follows:

2 People:
A shopkeeper refusing to sell you cigarettes in his shop.
Two wrestlers.
Saying goodnight to your girl/boy friend.
Having a talk with your social worker.

3 People:
Policemen arresting someone in the street.
A Mr Universe contest.
Playing Frisbee.
Getting served in a fish and chip shop.

4 People:
Escape from prison - 2 prisoners, 1 warden, 1 dog.
A team of acrobats.
Closing time in a pub - 1 barman, 3 customers.
A court proceeding or children's hearing.

5 People:
A pop group.
Your own group.
People at a football match.
Making a film - 1 director, 1 camera operator, 3 actors.

Players should be numbered off e.g. 1-15, and corresponding cards are put in an envelope. The person introducing the game picks out a mime card at random and then takes out as many numbers from the envelope as are necessary to do the mime. People whose number comes up must leave the room to rehearse their mime. On their return, the mime is performed in front of the group - it can be treated purely and simply as a bit of fun for participants and spectators, or the group may get more involved and can be asked to guess what the mime is.

This type of sequence is very popular, and always produces a few laughs. On the growth side, it is excellent for encouraging self-confidence and co-operative activity skills. Allow half an hour or so.

SITUATIONS

An immensely useful discussion technique which encourages the group to look at particular social situations, and how effectively individuals cope with them. The technique is capable of infinite adaptation and can be used with adult training groups as well as with young people. It can be a useful way to introduce tricky issues and dilemmas in a family group. Suitable for small groups only; the 'situations' are prepared in advance,and written out on cards. 20 cards should suffice for a small group.

Examples of thought-provoking situations are:

'What would you do if your teacher accuses you of stealing something from the classroom. It wasn't you but you know who it was.'

'What would you do if you find out that a friend of yours has been experimenting with drugs?'

'What would you do if a friend comes to you and says he has committed a serious assault and wants you to hide him from the police?'

Players should select a card in turn round the group. Each person can be asked to state how they would handle the situation and then the issue can be discussed by the whole group. The group leader should encourage all group members to contribute their responses, being careful to stress that usually there is no 'one answer' to any particular situation.

A good sequence for increasing self-confidence and self-expression. 'Situations' can help establish group norms and stimulate increased awareness of 'difficult' adolescent experiences. Cards can be customised to raise issues which are 'live' for the group or individual members and this can often lead to an in-depth discussion arising. Allow at least half an hour.

COMPUTER

This is the classic relationship game for young people. It offers emotional stimulation and feedback, helps people communicate honestly with each other, and is adaptable for different ages and to the size and the maturity of the group. It is also tremendous fun to play!

Adults must be prepared to spend time preparing 'computer cards' for the sequence - and these can be easily designed to suit the particular characteristics of groups and their stages of development: **introductory, established and advanced**.

Some **examples** of cards are:

INTRODUCTORY
The person with the knobbiest knees
The cuddliest person
The person with the nicest smile
The person you'd most like to be locked in a dark room with
ESTABLISHED
The person you'd most like to have as your friend
The person who thinks they're a 'hard man', but aren't
The biggest scrounger
The person who usually gets a raw deal

ADVANCED
The most honest person
The person you've liked most this evening
The person who finds it hardest to tell the truth
The person who always gets it wrong !

The sequence commences with the person introducing the game asking for a volunteer to select a card. The card is not read aloud, but should be handed on by the volunteer to the person that it 'fits' best. So if the volunteer (in an established group) selects a card with 'the person who's annoyed you most this evening' on it, he might well give it to Alan - because he's been hassling him all evening. Alan must then read the card out loud to the group, return it to the pile and take his turn at selecting a card.

Players should be constantly encouraged to give their cards to the most appropriate person - and should be given feedback by the group as to the suitability of their choice. Some kids may need adult help to make the most appropriate choice, and this should be offered freely, until everyone is comfortable with the sequence.

Provided that you start a group off with introductory sequences, kids will rapidly get used to 'Computer', and will be prepared to debate, and ultimately accept as relevant, other people's perceptions of them. Moreover, this will take place in an atmosphere of mutual trust and enjoyment.

Computer is a relationship tool that can be constantly adapted as the group matures. It is worth spending a fair amount of time preparing the cards and designing them around your particular group's interests and attributes. Cards should ideally be hand-printed or typed so that they can be easily read, and help should be given discretely to anyone who has difficulty reading the cards. Adults should also be on the look-out for those who, towards the end of the sequence, have not yet received cards; does this mean that there has not been a suitable card for them, or have they been ignored for some other reason?

In an introductory version of 'Computer' the games leader would probably want to use any trick in the book to make sure that each player is offered a card, even if it's a nasty one! The same leader in an advanced group might want to ask them why Paddy hasn't had a card, and why all Mary's have been a bit brutal!

Computer is infinitely capable of adaptation - so much so that kids will often get into making their own sets of cards for parties or special group events. In an advanced group the sequence can be played with each person retaining the cards that have been given to them (instead of returning them to the pile). At the end of the game this enables the leader to invite people in turn to read out the cards they have received and so encourage discussion and debate.

The amount of material produced in an average computer session is immense, but it does take leadership skill, and the ability to recognise and use group dynamics, to enable young people to process this material productively. 'Computer', of course, should (like any other game) only be used in this way if it 'fits in' with the rest of the session, and the group's purpose.

It's possible for Computer to be played without cards in some advanced groups. This requires a volunteer to think of the first 'Computer' phrase, which is then whispered to the first player who must say it out loud to the most appropriate person in the group. The receiver of the phrase thinks of one to whisper to the next player, and so the sequence continues until everyone in the group has received at least one phrase.

Playing time in 'standard' versions is dependent on the number of cards prepared and the size of the group. Try to allow 2 or 3 cards for each person. It will probably fill at least 20-30 minutes.

FEAR IN THE HAT

This is a useful game for small group work and can easily be adapted to cover a range of emotions, e.g. 'Love in a Hat', 'Anger in a Hat', etc.

This sequence should only be attempted when you feel that the group members are at the stage where they will be prepared to share some of their emotions with one other. A game like this is a relatively easy way of introducing the idea of sharing emotions with friends and peers as an alternative to acting out or repressing strong emotional feelings.

The sequence will need some kind of introduction by an adult, which should ideally be related to some activity or discussion where the group can be asked to identify what triggers off a particular emotion during a discussion or activity. A pencil and a piece of paper are required for each person in the group, and the sequence commences with the leader asking the group to complete a sentence like:

'In this group I am afraid that....' (or in the case of 'Anger in a Hat', 'In this group I get angry when ....').

When everyone has completed their sentence, all the slips of paper should be put in a hat or similar receptacle. The receptacle

is then passed round the group to each person, in turn, who selects a slip of paper, reads it out and then elaborates on it trying to express exactly what the person who wrote it was feeling.

So, after reading out a slip of paper which says e.g. 'I am afraid that people slag (criticise) me', someone might say 'There's a lot of slagging in this group and that puts people off saying anything serious'. If the group find this kind of individual feedback too threatening, the leader can stimulate a group discussion on the various factors that have been identified as triggering off anger, criticism, scapegoating, fear, etc.

The usefulness of this type of sequence arises from the material that is produced during play. Role play can easily be used instead of discussion, and leaders might like to give some feedback on the dynamics of the group, relating this also to emotional responses. It must be remembered that this style of groupwork necessitates adults sharing their own emotional responses with young people in the group. Allow up to 45 minutes.

CHINESE ROULETTE

At least half an hour is needed for this guessing game. Because it involves describing characteristics of other group members, we would always classify it as a sequence for well-established groups. The game was used in an epic of the modern German cinema to illustrate the lack of communication and understanding within a group.

To start, one member of a group (there should be at least 5 for a good game) volunteers to answer questions pretending that they are another member of the group. The volunteer does not indicate who they are trying to be, and each group member in turn, asks one question which the volunteer tries to truthfully answer in the style of the chosen person. The game can be played with either one or two rounds of questions being asked, followed by a round of guesses, where each group member says who they think has been portrayed. They can, of course, say that it is themselves!

The style of the questions is important to the game and the best types of question are along the following lines:
> 'If you were a colour, what would you be?' or 'If you were going to commit suicide, how would you do it?' or 'What sort of flower would you be?'

It's an interesting and varied game and it makes considerable demands on the person who is answering the questions. They must try really hard to get 'inside' their chosen person, since the questions will relate to matters not normally considered. Making sure that everyone has been chosen as the subject is impossible, but the whole group should feel involved since the sequence has a high 'games' level. Was it Alan or Howie who was the Venus-Flytrap?

PERSONAL STATEMENTS

'Personal Statements' is an excellent device for providing feedback, both positive and negative, to individual members of a small or large group. It is used most constructively by groups at an advanced stage of development, although the game can be used with groups who have not yet reached this stage by insisting that, e.g. only positive statements are made.

The person introducing the game should explain that one person is required to leave the group and go out of earshot. The remaining members of the group then suggest various statements which could be made about the person outside the group. The three most appropriate (or humorous! - with a less advanced group) are written down or committed to memory by e.g. the group leader. The person outside is then invited to come back into the group and listen to the three statements which have been made about them. They must then try to guess who made each of the statements. When this sequence has been completed the leader should nominate someone else to leave the group, and the sequence can continue until each person has had a chance to have statements made about them.

If the game is being played competitively, then the winner is the person who has the most correct guesses. (Allow 3 guesses at theauthor of each statement.) Workers' attitudes and responses are important in this game to make sure that the game is used in a positive way. The usual practice is to suggest to the group that they make a couple of positive statements about each person and one critical (but honest) one. There are obvious opportunities for using personal statements in a small group as a personality feedback exercise, although this should only be done where the group leader is convinced that players are mature enough to handle this kind of issue. Allow 30 minutes' playing time minimum.

TRUTH, DARE, DOUBLE DARE, PROMISE, REPEAT, KISS, COMMAND

Most people will have played this game at some point in their youth, and should therefore be familiar with its concept. The sequence contains some of the challenging aspects of games like 'The Truth Game' and 'Computer', but there is a freedom of choice present which enables individuals to participate at different levels. The 'difficult' categories for adolescents are likely to be:
'Truth'; 'Double Dare'; 'Kiss'; and 'Command'.

Seven sets of cards are required - the sequence can be played with less, but this does restrict the range of choice. Some examples of suitable cards are as follows:

TRUTH: The question on the card must be answered truthfully.

Is it true that you are lonely sometimes?
Is it true that you are shy with girls/boys?
Is it true that your best friend sometimes lets you down ?

DARE: You must do what the card says.

I dare you to take off two articles of clothing.
I dare you to pretend you are having a shower.
I dare you to pretend you are a dog.

DOUBLE DARE: The person in charge of the cards must also do what the card says.

I double dare you to roll your trousers up to the knee for the rest of the game.
I double dare you to crawl on your hands and knees right round the room.
I double dare you to pick a partner and do a wee dance.

PROMISE: This often applies to the future.

Promise to kiss someone good-bye when you leave the group tonight.
Promise to sing a song once the game is finished.
Promise to hold hands with someone till the game ends.

REPEAT: The words on the card must be repeated as fast as possible.

Repeat 3 times:
'The Leith police dismisseth us.'

Repeat 3 times:
'I'm not a pheasant plucker, I'm a pheasant plucker's son, and I'm only plucking pheasants till the pheasant plucker comes.'

Repeat 3 times:
'If Peter Piper picked a peck of pickled pepper, where's the peck of pickled pepper Peter Piper picked?'

KISS: You must carry out the action specified on the card.

Give the person sitting on your right a peck on the cheek.
Ask the nearest person of the opposite sex to give you a kiss.
Pretend you are kissing the person of your dreams in the back row of the pictures.

COMMAND: More difficult than a dare, and the action must be carried out.

I command you to stand back to back with some

friendly person and give each other a cuddle.
I command you to go up to someone you fancy and ask
them to give you a big cuddle.
I command you to sit on the floor for the rest of the
game.

Try to make up at least six cards in each of the seven categories - this will be more than enough for most small groups, and just about adequate for a large one. Like computer cards, these can be made more difficult and challenging to suit the ongoing development of the group - but don't forget the 'funnies', as this keeps the interest level high.

One person in the group must take charge of the cards - remember that if anyone selects a Double Dare card, then the person in charge of the cards must perform the action as well. Initially, it may be best if the cards are held by an adult. The sequence commences with someone selecting one card from any of the seven bundles and following the instruction on the card. Thereafter, people should take a card in turn round the group. Players should be encouraged to carry out the action and not 'pass', although it can be an idea to let the group know which are the easier categories.

'Truth, Dare, Double Dare, Promise, Repeat, Kiss, Command' should only be used with an established group. You will probably find that the group themselves will eventually be quite strict about not allowing people to 'pass', and might even want to institute a system of penalties. This is O.K. as long as 'execution' and assault and battery are all discouraged!

You may need to limit the time the group spends on this game - it can be very popular and we have known of instances where groups have literally spent hours playing it. The sequence is very well suited for large groups, but can be fun for smaller ones too.

THE TELEPHONE GAME

This is a spectator-type game which is best used with an advanced group. If kids are into playing this particular game, the results can be absolutely hilarious.

Much beloved of Panmure House in Edinburgh, the Telephone Game is usually played at the end of a session with a large group. It is eminently suitable for those youngsters who have a spark of showmanship, and who can rarely find a constructive outlet for their talent!

As a spectator exercise, it can work with as few as three or four people completing the sequence. As the game is used progressively during the life of a group, it will be found that other youngsters and adults can build up the appropriate skills required to make utter and complete idiots of themselves in front of the rest of the group!

Ideally, the game should be played with the group sitting in a semi-circle with one empty chair in the centre. A volunteer is required to choose a card which has on it something like:
> 'I am a sex maniac' or 'Is that why you phoned me at this time of night?', 'I love you', 'You really piss me off' etc.

The volunteer sits on the seat in the middle facing the group and pretends to be talking on the telephone to anyone of their choosing. However, they must end their conversation with the phrase on the card - and must try to have an imaginary conversation which makes some kind of sense. The sequence can be repeated as many times as there are volunteers.

An essential part of any spectator sequence is that the group should be helped to provide encouragement for the person in the middle - who is, after all, providing free entertainment for everyone else! Adults can help in this process, and might like to show off their own acting talents in the sequence to provide a model for young people to copy and adapt.

SURVIVORS

'Survivors' is a small group role-play technique which usually produces lively discussion. It places the group in the rather nasty situation where one person has to be sacrificed so that the rest can survive. The group task is to choose the most expendable person, and this is usually done by discussion which is centred on the various roles which have been ascribed to group members.

As with any role play, you should set the scene carefully and encourage the group to think themselves into the situation. Explain that the group are survivors of some kind of holocaust - a hurricane or a nuclear explosion - and this has brought them together for the first time.

If it is a hurricane, this will have led to them being adrift at sea on a raft which will only continue to float if one person jumps overboard to certain death in the shark-infested waters. In the aftermath of a nuclear explosion, the group will have gathered together ina nuclear shelter where they will have to stay for a month until radiation levels are low enough to leave. Unfortunately, one person must leave the shelter immediately so that the air and rations will last out for the month.

Cards can be used to ascribe roles to players, e.g. farmer, doctor, labourer, social worker, plumber, scientist, etc. Tell the group that they must decide which person to sacrifice on the basis of the importance of each person's contribution to the new society. The leader should stress that drawing lots or volunteering is not allowed. So, the group not only has to agree on who to sacrifice, they have to decide on how to make that decision - open vote, closed ballot etc. Adults in the group should participate fully in the role play, and can provide a useful lead to others by adding depth to their particular character, e.g. a self-important scientist, an outraged businessman, etc.

'Survivors' can be an experience in itself, but has obvious potential as a lead-in to group discussions on societal roles, group decision making etc. Due to its relatively unstructured nature, 'Survivors' should only be introduced when the group feels secure with role-play techniques. Allow 20 minutes to half an hour minimum, after the introduction.

STORYTELLING

Verbal confidence can be built up using this sequence. Ideal for small groups, or as a spectator experience with 7 or 8 people from a large group. The aim of the game is to improvise a story, with each person telling a bit of it. The person introducing the game might want to start the story themselves, or nominate an adult to begin, so that players have an idea of what is expected from them.

The person starting the sequence should begin to tell a story, and should stop whenever they like; the person on their right must then continue the story for a bit before stopping and handing over to the next person to the right, and so on around the group until the story is finished.

If necessary, the leader can suggest a theme for the story, to make things easier e.g. a robbery, a love story etc. The material produced in story telling can be used for an improvised drama session, or can be tape recorded and played back to the group for their amusement. The leader might also want to initiate some kind of feedback session on individual performances, as the storyteller's expertise and confidence can be further built up in this way. The sequence itself can be repeated as required . Allow 10 minutes or so for each story.

THE SILENCE GAME

Very much a small group experience for advanced groups of older adolescents, the Silence Game is a useful tool for stimulating discussion on non-verbal communication, group norms, personal limits etc.

The aim of the game, simply put, is for the group to maintain absolute silence for as long as possible. The gaming element involves each group member writing down on a piece of paper the name of the person they think will be first to break the silence. Each player's own name should be written in a corner of the paper to enable discussion on e.g. who chose whom and why. This discussion can be initiated as soon as the silence is broken.

Care should be taken to ensure that the group will be left alone and without interruption for the duration of the game. The sequence is particularly useful for eliciting comment on what it feels like to be a member of the group in the absence of any verbal interaction. Discussion can be stimulated by questions like:
> *'Did you feel uncomfortable with the silence?', 'What were you thinking about?', 'Did your thoughts stay in the room, or were you thinking about things outside the room?'*

Just in case you happen to get lumbered with an exceptionally determined group of young people, it is best to state a maximum time limit for the silence exercise. 10-15 minutes is probably a realistic maximum.

BRAINSTORMING AND QUESTIONNAIRES

These are not games as such but have been included in this section because they are basic groupwork techniques which can be used to produce a multitude of material for group discussion.

Brainstorming has the effect of encouraging group cohesion by valuing each member's contribution equally. It creates a collaborative atmosphere rather than a competitive one. A blackboard and chalk, and/or a flipchart and felt pen is necessary. The group can practise brainstorming by trying to imagine as many uses as possible for, e.g. a coke bottle, a shoe etc. The leader writes down the ideas as they are called out, omitting none. Everyone is encouraged to put in their own ideas and therefore remain a contributing member of the group. Two or three minutes should be allowed for the brainstorming sequence, after which the group can discuss the ideas produced, perhaps with a view to identifying the most practical ones.

With a large group, brainstorming can be played as a team game, each team having a leader. At the end of the session, the total for each team is announced. Teams can then be asked to decide in groups on their 5 or 10 most original ideas, and awarded points for ones not thought of by the other team.

Brainstorming can be used to help solve problems facing the group, e.g. 'Where should we go for our camping weekend?', we do to make the group more exciting?' etc. The technique can also be used to introduce the group to broad concepts by asking e.g. 'If you were given £500,000 to spend on a new facility for the community, what would you spend it on?' Brainstorming can be used with any size of group at all stages of development.

Questionnaires are useful tools in initiating discussion on personal and relationship issues. Suitable only for small groups where initial trust has been established; care should be taken to guard against difficulties arising from any group members who lack proficiency in reading or writing. Questionnaires must be prepared in advance and should be as simple as possible with participants being asked e.g. to fill in a missing word, or tick the appropriate box. Adults in the group should participate fully and honestly in filling in their own questionnaires.

Discussion can be initiated by exchanging questionnaires with the person on your right or left, and asking for both individual and group comment on particular responses. Try questionnaires like:

I am ....
I think ....
I want ....
I feel ....
I need .... etc.
I am .... at home
I am .... at school
I am .... in the group
I am .... with my friends etc.

FINGER LIFT

It is hard to describe the 'Finger Lift' without a diagram, so here goes!

The person to be levitated is seated and asked to relax. Four levitators (group members) then use the forefingers of both hands to try and lift the subject. The lifting points are under the thighs, behind the knees and under the armpits. Not too smelly, we hope!

On a pre-arranged signal, all the lifters use their two-fingered contact with the levitee (is there such a word?) and up the subject

goes, but not very smoothly or very well. The subject is returned, gently to their chair, and at this point we include a touch of mysticism. Each lifter, in clockwise direction, places one hand, palm downwards above the head of the person to be lifted. In this way, the hands are placed at about 1" distance from one another and form an 'aura of power' above the recipient's head until all 8 hands are displayed in this formation. Then slowly, one hand at a time from the top is withdrawn. The 4 lifters again take up positions using their two forefingers, and this time, miraculously, the person is lifted smoothly and easily and even 15 stone+ individuals 'float' towards the ceiling.

Don't ask us how or why it works this way, but work it does and all the participants get quite an electric buzz from the experience. The exercise is best undertaken with adolescent age-groups. From our experience, you may find yourself with a queue of eager participants and don't be too surprised if the staff members find themselves nearer the stars during the session in which the 'Finger Lift' is tried out!

THE TRUTH GAME

There is more than one version of this 'heavy' sequence. It can be played in mixed adult/kids' groups, but we found that adults felt especially threatened by the exercise and in one conference we attended, two adult staff walked out of the group. The game can last for more than one 2 hour session, or it can be scaled down to about an hour/hour and a half. It is useful if everyone can be given a stretch in the 'hot seat' being questioned by the rest of the group.

To start, one person volunteers to be questioned. One question is asked of this person and they must then answer as truthfully as possible. At this point all the group can join in, asking subsidiary questions to the original. This process, when the game is played at its heaviest, continues until the whole group is satisfied that the question has been fully answered. The sequence then restarts with the last person who was interrogated being allowed to choose the new victim and pose the questions.

Because the exercise relies on sharing one's personal life with the group, the level of aggression must be tempered with a high level of caring and sensitivity; making sure that everyone has made themselves vulnerable is one such means of ensuring that justice has been seen to be done.

The sort of questions which will inevitably be used will concern personal and sexual behaviour. Because of 'professional' veneer and feelings of vulnerability, the adult participants in the group will be more likely to lie and misrepresent themselves. A strong (but participating) chairperson is needed!

Variations

A faster sequence, based on the same principle, is to use either cards or a 'one question rule' around the group. To amplify:

With cards

A pile of cards is placed in the middle of the group and each person in turn picks a card, reads it out and tries to answer truthfully. *'What is the worst thing you've ever done?'* is the sort of pro forma. If a person cannot or does not want to answer the question they have received, they can miss a turn.

Two or more sets of cards can be used, e.g. Personal, General, Work, School, etc., thus giving players the opportunity of choosing particular areas (and therefore the degree of threat).

Verbally

A volunteer starts by asking a question of the person on their left. That person answers, and then asks the person on their left a question and so on around the group. If someone says 'pass' they forfeit their turn to ask a question.

THE RACK

The Rack is a very powerful sequence which should only be attempted with the most advanced small groups. It uses the adolescents' tendency to criticise their peers, and takes this to its limit. It is therefore unwise to attempt this sequence until such time as the group have discussed this behaviour, and come to an awareness of the social contexts in which critical, negative and generally abusive behaviour takes place.

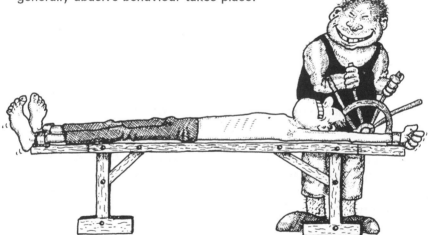

The person introducing 'The Rack' should spend some time preparing the group for it, stressing that it is an exercise in self-control which allows each individual to experience a whole range of negative feelings about them, expressed by the rest of the group, in the knowledge that these do not outweigh the positive feelings.

Each person in the group (including adults) takes it in turn to either sit in a chair in the centre of the circle, or lie stretched out on the floor. At a signal from the games leader, the person in the middle is put on the rack for a minute or a minute and a half. This involves the other group members trying every verbal thing they can think of to make the victim 'crack'. It is essential that the group spends time with each person immediately after they have been on the rack, discussing the feelings generated during the experience and whether or not it was found to be difficult.

'Rack-type' situations can arise spontaneously during the life of a group, and some workers will feel that they want to exploit this to the full. It is possible to introduce 'The Rack' when this occurs as long as the group is at an appropriate stage of development. However, bearing in mind the emotional stimulus that will have resulted in a spontaneous 'Rack' occurring, there is no guarantee that the experience will not backfire. Such spontaneous use is probably best left until the group have experienced, and are at ease with, 'The Rack'.

THE GOOD AND THE BAD

A very demanding sequence which requires a high degree of trust and honesty between participants. Its use with a small group should be carefully planned and adults should note that this is a difficult sequence, even for an advanced group.

The sequence itself is very simple to organise. As an introduction, The Good and the Bad can be likened to the 'Truth Game', i.e. players must agree to tell the truth before the sequence commences. The 'truth' element involves each person stating one thing they like about the person on their left, and one thing that they don't like.

Although a volunteer can be asked to start the sequence, it is particularly appropriate in this instance for an adult to go first, thus demonstrating that adults will be just as involved and honest as the kids. The games organiser's role is crucial in 'The Good and the Bad', as the onus is on him or her to 'freeze' the game and invite group members to comment on a particular individual's statements - or to ask about feelings generated by specific comments. This quality of intervention demands an intimate knowledge of the group and its process.

Used sensitively, this sequence has a great deal of potential, as long as workers are prepared to constructively use the material produced. Allow at least 30-45 minutes.

ALPHABET GAME

This is a wonderful game for involving all the participants, though it is best played with a group who have the confidence to be foolish in front of one another. There are plenty of variations as your group gets to know the game and enough scope for innovation, so use the basic rules as a 'starter' pack.

Ask a member of the group to start, giving them a letter to commence with, for instance, 'D'. This letter should then be used by the 'volunteer' as the starting letter of a song title, or first letter of the first line of a song which they then sing. The result might be a most original version of 'Doo Wah Diddy' or 'Don't Cry for Me Argentina'. There's lots of scope and it's best played at quite a fast pace. The next person tries 'E' and so on right round the group until the alphabet is exhausted.

If the players are not exhausted, try introducing new rules, for example, have a round where everyone has to sing a song starting with the same letter. Another variation is to choose songs with a theme. Titles or first lines with a 'colour' in them - 'Song Sung Blue'; 'Tie a Yellow Ribbon' etc.; or perhaps animals - 'I Do Like That Doggy in the Window'; 'Nellie the Elephant', 'Crocodile Rock' etc. There are lots of good subjects and it is a highly enjoyable sequence with most groups aged from about 11 or 12 years old. The group size can be anything from 4 to about a dozen. If you want to introduce rather a 'wicked' rule, allow players to sing out of turn, interrupting the player whose turn it is, thereby preventing particular songs from being used. To avoid tension, if some players are not so quick, allow 'helping out' with titles where necessary.

BLIND WALK

This sequence should only be used with groups which have established a high degree of trust. As with most trust sequences, you should have extra adults on hand to cover the safety aspects.

A volunteer is required who is blindfolded in the centre of the room, while the other players scatter themselves around the playing area. The blindfolded person is instructed to walk in as confident a way as possible around the room (not that easy when you're blind) while the other players stop the volunteer bumping into chairs, walls and other obstacles.

A **variation** requires people to walk in pairs - one person is blindfolded while the second acts as a guide who assists in negotiating stairs and other obstacles. When using the variation you should allocate an adult to monitor each pair's activities, or run the sequence as a spectator event with only one pair active at any one time.

It is essential to debrief after 'Blind Walk' - the exercise can be used to stimulate discussion on how we take our senses for granted, and is of obvious benefit in helping young people consider the plight of people with a physical impairment. A high level of trust and co-operation is needed for a successful 'Blind Walk' and discussion on these issues can easily be generated. Allow 15-20 minutes for the activity, prior to debriefing.

GIE ME FIVE!

Translated from Scots into English, this translates as 'GIVE ME FIVE! Although it probably exists elsewhere, this version was devised by Alex Stevens as a group consensus tool when working in a Drop-in Centre in Greenock. It's an excellent technique for structuring a group's decision-making.

Let's assume that you want a group of eight to agree on five things that they want to change about their group:

1. Ask each person to list the 5 things they want to change.

2. Create pairs and ask each pair to discuss the 10 things they have listed, and agree on 5 (allow 5 minutes).

3. Combine the pairs into two groups of four and go through the same process, i.e. discuss the 10 issues and agree on 5 (allow 10 minutes).

4. Now bring the two groups together into one group of eight and repeat the process, ending up with 5 things agreed by the whole group (allow 20 minutes).

Voila! You have an agreement on five things that everyone thinks should be changed.

The way you will manage this sequence depends on the number of people in the large group. For example, with 12 people you could either:

(a) Work in ones, pairs, fours, and then bring the three groups together .... but they will have to discuss 15 items rather than 10. Or,

(b) Work in threes, sixes, then twelve.

If you have an odd number in the group, say 15, you would work in ones, 6 pairs and a 3, 3 fours and a 3, a 3 and a 7, etc.

'Gie Me Five' works well with groups of adolescents and is an excellent technique when used in staff training sessions and staff team meetings to identify areas of agreement or priority. You should be aware, however, that although this process helps a group to agree on its' 5 priority issues, all other issues are lost. If it is important that all the ideas generated are considered by the group, then the next technique (The Consensus Game) is the one to use.

THE CONSENSUS GAME

This technique is relatively straightforward. It requires initial active collaboration from participants and it enables groups to tackle many issues in which a 'consensus' of opinion is required.

Materials: *Large pieces of 'brainstorming' paper.*
                   5 postcard size (or smaller) pieces of paper for

each participant.
Pens and Bluetack, etc.

Process: *1) Give everyone 5 pieces of card.*
2) Ask them to write 5 objectives they
personally find the most important to the issue
under discussion, one on each piece of card.
3) Having done this, place all responses on the
floor or a large table, face up, and ask all to
consider every statement. Then select the three
cards which are most important to them. (Be sure
to remove any duplicate cards prior to inviting
people to select their three).
4) Then, having established the prioritised list, i.e.
all the sets of three:
(a) Discard the unselected statements.
(b) Replace the sets of three on the floor or
table.
(c) Consider (10 mins.) all the statements.

After reading, and understanding all statements, (ask the author(s)
for clarification if required), ask everyone to turn over any that
they consider to be:

> *(a) Contrary to what they believe.*
> *(b) Need further clarification or discussion.*
> *(c) Of uncertain value*

Once this has been done:

> *(i) Remove all cards which are face down. Keep*
> *these cards.*
> *(ii) Recruit a volunteer to write up on brainstorm*
> *sheets all the remaining responses.*

These form the basis of a consensus of opinion on whatever
subject is being debated.

Important: Take the other cards and one by one debate whether or
not they should join the list or be discarded.

This game can be used in many ways, e.g. establishing a
programme for a group; establishing objectives for a project;
prioritising areas of work; looking at problems. Only suitable for

established groups of young people, 'The Consensus Game' can also be used as an excellent resource for staff development and training.

SKILLS WALL

An ideal technique for groups who wish to analyse the skills necessary for performing complex tasks. Useful when used with well established groups of adolescents, it comes into its own as a staff training tool. You'll need some flipchart paper, felt markers, index cards and pens. Brainstorming is used at the beginning of the exercise to identify the list of needs required to perform the particular task under discussion (see page 110).

The leader should help individuals to be specific about the needs they are identifying and write each one up on the sheets of flipchart paper. For example, with a group of young people wanting to plan a residential weekend, one of the needs might be 'someone who can drive the van' or 'someone who knows how to put a tent up'. With a group of staff who wish to involve volunteers in their work, a need might be 'someone who can offer support to the volunteers' or, 'someone who can plan a training course for them'.

Once the list of needs for the specific task is complete, give each member of the group some index cards, or similar, and ask them to write down all the skills they possess, one on each card. With young people especially, clarify exactly what a 'skill' is. Once all the skill cards are complete, pin them up on a wall some distance away from the list of needs.

Now comes the interesting bit .... ask the group to form a line from the 'needs wall' to the 'skills wall'. Starting with the person nearest to the 'needs wall', individuals pin each of their 'skill' cards against an appropriate need. You'll find, especially with groups of staff, that they actually possess all, or most of the skills necessary to meet the needs (usually without having realised it).

If there are gaps in the skills required to meet particular needs, these are now highlighted and the group can go on to discuss how to acquire the necessary skills to enable them to complete their task. With a staff team, this part is best carried out in small groups of 3 or 4 people, where individuals can support each other in discussing who could/should acquire particular skills. Allow up to one and a half hours for the complete exercise.

THE WIND UP

As with 'Levitation' and the 'Finger Lift' described elsewhere, this is a silly sequence which usually works and keeps folks amused. The actual basis of the puzzle is that muscles tire quite quickly, even in fit, healthy people-but you don't tell the person you are challenging that!

What you say is that you want the person to place the palms of their hands together and then interlock all their fingers, leaving the index, (fore) fingers sticking up. You continue by requesting that they keep their upright fingers about a quarter of an inch apart.

Now we reach the 'Wind-Up'. You take a bit of time explaining that you are going to be winding an invisible handle, which will force their fingers together, and that they must make every effort to resist you.

As long as you take your time spinning out the challenge, the muscles will tire and the fingers will move magically together!

PARTING GIFTS

This game is used towards the end of a group's life and it is used to help individuals express the support and understanding they have received from others in the group. Our friend, Tracey Hunter uses this technique extensively with groups of young people in Scotland, and also with adults in training situations - it's an excellent way of providing positive feedback at the end of training sessions.

You'll need a piece of flipchart paper, or similar, for each person in the group - each piece of paper should have a group member's name written on it. Spread the paper around the floor of the room and invite people to write down what each person has given them in terms of support, humour, understanding etc.

Encourage people to write a comment on each person's sheet. If the adult leader of the group has done their job as a facilitator well during the group's life, then group members will be able to recognise one another's positive qualities without difficulty. Stress to the group that it is a good thing for everyone to recognise each other's positive qualities, and to take the time to do this properly.

Debriefing involves the leader inviting people to move round the room to read the comments on each person's sheet. The leader may want to invite comments on how helpful/unhelpful people have been with one another generally or highlight particularly important incidents. Used in sequence with 'Picture Yourself', this technique helps demonstrate the personal gains individuals have made and how much they have moved on. Allow about 30 - 45 minutes with a small group.

Notes.

Section Five:
ETHNIC GAMES

A FEW SUGGESTIONS ON RUNNING GAMES SESSIONS

The following are possible 'Starters' as kids arrive:

For about half
an hour:

Ethnic games	Commercial games
Pool	Lego
Darts	Boggle
Marbles	Water games
Cards	Mazes
	Computer games (if available)

The above format is a useful one to start off with, if the group has a suitable place to meet. The lack of such a base need not be a major hurdle to overcome, as all the above games (excepting pool) are easily transportable, and can be set up and used almost anywhere.

We chose the combination of what we call 'Ethnic' and Commercial Games, as they cater for groups as well as one to one interaction. Young people in the group can therefore find themselves involved in several different types of gaming situations in a half hour period e.g. Sandy might have a game of 8 ball pool (doubles) with three other people, moving on to building a toppling space station with lego, which can easily involve two or three working in teams.

Using games in this context, workers can allow kids who are new to the group to experience enough space to make choices about the kind of game they play and the number of people they get involved with at any particular time. Our selection of Ethnic/Commercial Games will be known to most young people and this should help allay any uncomfortable feelings which might otherwise be generated in introductory sessions by 'pushing' games which are unfamiliar.

Should this kind of opener to an I.T. session or a youth club evening become a regular feature, one would expect the inclusion of some unfamiliar games, and an emphasis on encouraging the group to try, for example: Rotation Pool, Shanghai Darts, Switch, Spoons, etc.

Prior to any session involving games, workers should consider their response to young people who are non-participators. Adults generally find it extremely difficult to understand and work with the (quite common) adolescent response of "I'm not going to play your ****** silly games".

Much will depend on the expectations that kids have of the sessions, and any contracts or agreements they have made with workers. Also, and importantly, much will depend on the example set by the adults in leading by getting involved.

If, for example, games are to be a regular feature of the sessions and kids have 'contracted-in' to the group on this understanding, then the response quoted above is clearly unreasonable, and this should of course be discussed with the non-participator. The ultimate worker response will depend on a number of variables, which are beyond the scope of this publication, e.g. overall aims and objectives of sessions; personal and group boundaries; interactional skills of workers; group decision-making/sharing processes, etc. There's a world of difference between the classroom, the youth club, the I.T./Social Work Group, and the family.

We would like to state that the idea of forcing anyone to participate in games is anathema to us .... games should be fun and participation should be voluntary. Some young people, however, will need to be encouraged in a variety of ways. This can be exceptionally difficult where a young person's past experiences have not, for whatever reason, included play as a life skill, or where particular kinds of play, e.g. physical/exuberant, have been discouraged.

Workers should find the various sections in the New Youth Games Book helpful in designing sessions which will be attractive to non-participators. There is obvious potential in our introductory half hour, for a worker to be equipped with a number of techniques which might facilitate this.

Puzzles and two-player games could be used for this purpose, e.g. Triangles, One in the Middle, The Football Team. Visually interesting equipment like Water Games and Lego can also be used to encourage non-participators. Some will be quite happy to participate on their own by e.g. using a maze, or playing a computer game

Electronic Pin-ball tables are renowned in youth social work circles for their potential as one player games which can keep group non-participators happily occupied without feeling excluded from the group gaming. Expensive pieces of equipment they might be, but a tremendous resource if you can get hold of one. They can also be social places where conversation is easier than sitting around a table. Similarly, a table-football machine is a good fun way of relaxing and playing together. In the home, a small snooker table, darts or even a table tennis table might provide a similar meeting place for shared relaxation and enjoyment.

Games sequences can be used at various points in any particular session, e.g., as an introduction to the session, or to round it off well. Games can also be heavily used on special occasions like parties and visitors' nights. We think that it is worthwhile to encourage groups to gather together at the end of an evening to play games and thus share an enjoyable experience, whether it's Unihoc, Computer or Burma Road.

DARTS

Darts is perhaps the standard pub game. It is also one of the traditional pieces of equipment possessed by most youth centres, alongside the table-tennis table and some form of snooker or pool table. Said to have been invented by two Royalist officers during the Civil War period and played in a convenient pub, its ownership has also been claimed by Sussex folk, who in the 19th century were still playing 'pug-darts', a game where a small dart was projected through a blow-pipe at a four and a half inch diameter board. Whatever its history, the game is now popular throughout Britain and except for a brief period in the 1940s when some Scottish magistrates tried to ban the game because they claimed that it encouraged "ne'er do wellism", the game has been well patronised by all sections of the community.

The game itself is played on what is usually a standard board, 18 inches in diameter, with a set number sequence, 20 at the top, 3 at the bottom and with 'doubles' in a band at the outside of the scoring section of the board, a 'trebles' band midway to the centre (or bull) and the centre 'inner' and 'outer' which score 50 and 25 respectively. Other boards exist in different localities, ranging from the Yorkshire board, with its single bull, no trebles and diamond shapes between the 14 and 9 and the 4 and 13, through to the London Target board with its concentric rings, which, score between 0 and 100 as the arrow approaches the centre of the board. The Target board and the Narrow Five board (where all numbers are multiples of five, i.e. 5,10,15 or 20; singles, doubles, trebles) are both used for games where players aim to reach a set score, say 1,000 first, unlike the traditional standard game of darts which is a reduction from 1001, 501 or 301 down to '0', with the final score having to be achieved exactly.

The distance away from the board varies, regionally from 8 ft, 8 ft 6 ins to 9 ft. But whichever distance is taken, the players are expected to 'toe the line' and not encroach over it.

There are other 'special' dart boards on the market, designed for playing particular games such as 'golf', and 'cricket', but our aim is to suggest a variety of games which can be played using the standard dart board as the basic equipment. For games on the dart board, we would suggest using one of the 'fun' introductions for choosing who starts first. If it is a singles game, nearest bull wins and if it is a pairs game the pairs are chosen by a process where all 4 players throw for bull and then the nearest and furthest away are paired, leaving the two middle players as the second pair.

STANDARD DARTS

Tournament rules at a national level have been standardised, but the starting and finishing rules around the country vary.

To Start

After deciding whether the game is to be played in equal teams of more than 2 players a side, in pairs or singly, the starting total from which all subsequent scores are deducted, is established. As previously stated, this is normally 301, 501 or 1001.

In most places, play for an individual or team commences when they score a 'double'. From then on the aim is to reduce the starting score to zero in the fewest turns of 3 darts per go. Darts must remain sticking in the board for them to be counted and the player must toe the line for the go to be valid. To make the game a little easier for young people, you can play 'straight in' at the start, with players not requiring a double to start.

Scoring

In most places the score is kept on a chalk or dry board. If there is one available, the next challenger chalks the board and keeps score for the players either for one game or for a series of best of 3 games.

Finishing

When the player(s) reach a number of 50 or less, that is a double of another number on the board, they aim for that double and if successful that throw takes them to zero and they win. If, however, they miss, making their new total an odd number, they continue until a new double is obtained. In most areas, if a player throws and goes past the number required, the score returns to the one at the beginning of the go. (This is called going bust.)

So for example, a player aiming '40' who scores treble 20 returns to double top. In some areas, a 'no-bust' rule operates, meaning that if you find yourself going down from double 20, throw an odd number, say 21, leaving 19, you are not allowed to bust it to return to double 20 on the next turn. If you bust in this game you return to your last score, i.e.19,or whatever, rather than the score from the beginning of the turn. When a player reaches double one (the lowest double) if he or she misses the double and hits a single one, many players will allow the thrower one dart to 'split the 11', meaning attempting to get a dart between the two legs of the 11 on the wire. If the try is successful that player is adjudged to be the winner.

ROUND THE CLOCK

This is a game for individuals to practise their dart skills, or for a number of players. Everyone starts by aiming at No. 1 and then for No. 2, hitting numbers in order through to 20 or even to 50 (the bull). Usually an extra throw is allowed for players who score the number that they aim for with the last dart (third).

It is a useful introduction to the position of numbers on the board and not too difficult for the beginner. Whether you allow doubles and trebles to count is a question of 'local rules'. We usually allow them.

For a more advanced game, you can play all the way round on doubles and/or only allow an extra go if all three darts 'scored'.

KILLER DARTS

This is one of the most popular alternative games for use on the dart board. It is also one of the most fiendish, since the aim is to knock opponents off the board completely. If used in a youth group one must be careful that resentment does not run too high! It is a game for groups of 4 or more, so it fits the group work model well in terms of size if not in ethos.

To start, players throw one dart each with the hand they don't normally use, until they hit a number. That is then their number (unless it is already occupied) through until the end of the game. The game is then played using the normal hand, thus:

1) Each player tries to get exactly 5 of his or her number. (Doubles count x2; trebles x3.)

2) If a surplus is scored you reduce the score by the extra i.e. if, when a player already has four 3's they hit a treble 3, the score goes up 1 and down 2, so the end result is 3x threes, one down on the start!

3) Once a player has 5 of their number they are marked up as killer, which is normally written as I I I I K. They can then aim for any opponents' numbers. If the person they hit is killing, that person must then aim for their own number again before they are killer again. Numbers must be killed off exactly, or otherwise lives are given back.

4) If non-killers hit other players' numbers, apart from those killing, they can give lives to the opposition.

5) The winner is the last player left in.

There are a number of variations of this game, but this is the one we like best. Obviously, the game can be played using less lives, such that only '3' of a number are required to become killer. On the other end of the scale, the game could be revised using 'doubles' only - so 3 doubles, for instance, are needed before a person is killing.

SCRAM

This is played by two players. One player acts as 'STOPPER', the other is 'SCORER'. The Stopper throws first, normally aiming at the highest numbers first. (Bull is not used.) These numbers are counted as 'dead' once hit by the Stopper. The Scorer must then aim for other parts of the board and score the maximum points. Trebles and Doubles count. The game goes on until all numbers have been hit by the Stopper; the Scorer's total is fixed and roles reversed. The winner is the person who scores most as Scorer.

MICKEY MOUSE

This is usually played by two players, or two equal teams. The first requirement of this game is to chalk up a run of numbers on the blackboard e.g.

A								B
	I I I	20	I I I	
	I I I	19	I I I	
	I I I	18	I I I	
	I I I	17	I I I	
	I I I	16	I I I	
Score	I I I	15	I I I	Score
	I I I	14	I I I	
	I I I	13	I I I	
	I I I	12	I I I	
	I I I	11	I I I	
	I I I	10	I I I	
Total	I I I	B	I I I	

The marks to the left and right of the numbers represent the number of times each player has 'hit' the number in question (doubles and trebles count as 2x and 3x respectively). Once a player has 3 of a number, they are scoring on that number until the opponent 'closes' the number by getting their 3 of that number.

The game ends when all the numbers are closed and the winner is the player with the highest total.

This works best with players who are fairly used to playing darts or who are at the same standard of play.

FIVES

A very simple game which can be fun and doesn't require great skill. Any number from 2 upwards can play. Each player throws 3 darts and must get all 3 darts in the scoring part of the board. The aim is to score a total which is divisible by 5, then that number i.e. 40 ÷ 5 = 8 is scored. Play continues up to a pre-arranged total, normally 50 or 61. Scores not divisible by 5 are worthless. You can vary the game by scoring on numbers divisible by 5 and 3, which is perhaps easier with kids, although the scoring becomes more difficult. Thus 15 would score on 3s and 5s which gives (15 ÷ 3 = 5) + (15 ÷ 5 = 3) = 8 total.

DARTS FOOTBALL

There are various versions of this game, all normally for two players or for teams. The one we like best is a variant of 'Round The Clock'. Players choose whether their goal is No. 1 or No. 20. Then, after the toss of a coin (well, it is football!) one side kicks off. This is done by aiming at 11 if the player's goal is 1, and 10 if the goal is 20. From then on play proceeds up and down the number range of the board.

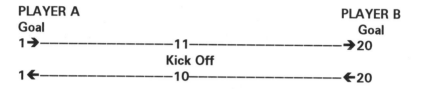

If, for instance, Player A scores 11 with the first dart, misses with the second and hits 12 (their direction of play) with the third, the player goes again; third dart scoring gives an extra go. Perhaps, only the second dart finds the 13 target in this go, so at this point play changes to Player B, who tries to move the ball in the opposite direction i.e. towards Player A's goal at No. 1. Player B must aim at the last number successfully hit by Player A, thus he or she takes up the ball by hitting point 13 and then aims for 12, 11, and so on in descending order. Play continues until a goal is scored, then another kick-off takes place. As a game, it is good practice and can be an absorbing way of spending half an hour

Alternatives are: Each player aims at the bull (inner or outer). Success gives control of the ball, allowing that player to shoot at doubles (goal). Each double is one goal and this barrage continues until the opponent regains possession by scoring a bull. Normally a ten goal limit determines the end of the game.

A strange 3rd variety of football is for experts only. Players aim for a number and once this has been determined, (They must both be different) each player shoots for a progression of segments. This is most easily explained in a diagram:

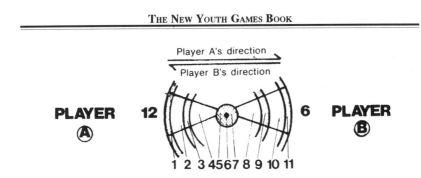

PLAYER Ⓐ 12 6 **PLAYER Ⓑ**

Player A's direction

Player B's direction

1 2 3 4567 8 9 10 11

Key:
Small numbers (1) etc. indicate the direction of play and segments which must be hit by Player A on the way towards Player B's goal at double 6. Player B's play is the exact reverse.

The first player to achieve hits at every segment en route is the winner. The 'third dart scoring' rule can be used to make the game more interesting.

BURMA ROAD

This is one of the 'greats', we think, for working with young people. It can be played with large groups which is often a godsend, if the dart board has suddenly become a popular place. First, a series of arbitrary numbers is chosen, normally including double, treble, bull and possibly a 'nominated number'. Each player then aims for each number or segment in turn. The scoreboard provides a clear explanation of what is happening. If a player fails to score with any of the 3 darts, then the cumulative total is halved (odd numbers count high).

A	B	score	C	D	E
20	–	20	20	40	100
10	2	2	22	44	102
16	59	T	11	22	129
20	63	4	31	26	65
35	93	15	106	13	80
75	99	D	53	39	40
81	123	6	59	45	20
121	143	Nom.	78	65	140
130	72	9	39	83	149
65	36	B	89	42	75

As you can see from the score sheet the game has skilful elements, but the lead can change very fast and the end is frequently a surprise, even to the myopic 7 year old who has just beaten their mum or dad, or the youth club leader who fancies himself a bit!

A rule that can be included is to say that all players must achieve some score in one of the first 3 rounds. Linked to this, the player who has reached a score of 1, stays put for 3 rounds before being eliminated.

SHANGHAI

This is a popular game and the scoring of a 'Shanghai' sometimes spills over into the Standard 301-type game. A Shanghai is to score a single, treble and double of any number in the same 3 darts. This can be used as an end game in standard darts if all contestants are agreed. It adds, like the 'split the 11' rule an extra fun element. If used in 301, it must be 'called' before the third dart is thrown.

Anyway, in this game the board is marked up as follows:

A	B	●	C	D
		1		
		2		
		③		
		4		
		5		
		6		
		⑦		
		8		
		9		
total	total		total	total
☐	☐		☐	☐

Each player throws 3 darts at each number in order, scoring the total. Doubles and Trebles count. 3's and 7's must be scored (if you are playing the 'serious' game) - failure means dropping out.

A Shanghai (double, treble, single), on the other hand, means outright victory. Otherwise the player with the highest total wins. This is a good game for groups of players, but perhaps the '3' and '7' drop out numbers - known as being 'Shanghaied' needs omitting with kids' groups.

DARTS CRICKET

This can be played by 2 players, or teams. One side 'bats', the other 'bowls'. In the version we prefer, the batting team scores as runs, everything scored above 40 (but they must not hit the inner or outer bull).

The bowlers try to hit the bull - inner counts two wickets (i.e. two batsmen out) and an outer as one wicket down. The scoreboard looks like:

At this point the score is 77 runs for 3 wickets.

A	B
卌卌lllll lllll	4 , 10, 15, 48,

After an innings, i.e. 11 or 10 wickets have fallen, the sides reverse roles and at the end of one or two innings for each side a victor is found.

Not a bad game, but it requires some skill from the bowlers, which can make it rather slow!

One additional rule which we have seen used is to count as runs to the batting team darts thrown by the bowling team which end up outside the treble ring. This gives just an ever so slight incentive to the bowlers to achieve accurate results!

LITTLE 'UNS 'N BIG 'UNS

This curiously titled game comes from Essex. Or, at least that's where we were first taught it. It's particularly useful for use with mixed size youth groups because it doesn't take much learning and any number can play.

Firstly, all the players' names are chalked or written up on a board. Then a number, or rather a segment of a number is chosen for starting. We suggest that this is done by one player randomly throwing a dart up at the board with their 'non-throwing' arm. Wherever this lands is the number and segment of the board which the next player must aim at. So, for instance, the dart may fall in a treble 4. The next player throws 3 darts at treble 4. Any hitting treble 4 score 3x4. After the three darts, if they've scored, they throw one dart at any other section of the board for the next player to aim at. If they fail to hit the target with their three darts, the next player also has to aim at the same number and the first player is knocked out. Play continues in order until only one player remains. The person with the highest score wins.

And, why is it called 'Little 'Uns 'n Big 'Uns' you're asking, aren't you? Well, if the dart goes into the section of the board between the double and treble, that's a 'Big 'Un', i.e. a Big 5, or whatever. Similarly, a 'Little 'Un' is the segment between the treble and Bull.

NOUGHTS AND CROSSES

If you want a game that is easy to explain and immediately appeals to youngsters, try this one! The noughts and crosses grid is drawn up with numbers from the dart board written in to the squares. It's for 2 players or teams of equal numbers.

i.e. at its simplest:

1	2	3
4	5	6
7	8	9

Players either aim for 'singles' of each number, or for more interest value, 'doubles' of the numbers concerned. As numbers are hit, the numbers are replaced by noughts and crosses. Thus:

X	X	Ø
4	5	Ø
X	8	Ø

with the 'noughts' player having scored on 3, 6 & 9.

A more advanced version can be played using the Bull (inner or outer) for the centre squares. So that the grid becomes:

17	2	4
11	B	5
9	3	20

DOMINOES

If you didn't know it, there are not always 28 dominoes (stones, blocks, tiles or bones) in a pack. The set beginning with a double blank and running through all the possibilities to double six is the most common, but you may stumble across any size of pack up to double twelves, which would give you 91 tiles - rather a large number for the normal coffee table !

Anyway, we have assumed that you are the proud possessors of the double-six pack and that you have always been afraid of displaying your singular lack of knowledge in front of the youngsters.

Games can be played by anything from 2 upwards. If 'partnerships' are involved then they can be decided by agreement or by drawing from the pack. The two players with the 'heaviest' dominoes (i.e. the highest numerical value) then form a pair. Partners normally sit opposite each other. Play proceeds with each player following on with matching dominoes corresponding with the number at one or other end of the line. We are not convinced that it is the best of all group games, therefore we only include a limited variety of alternatives. However, having said that, if you ever work with any ethnic groups of people, you will have to learn their variety of domino games, since they vary considerably around the world..

THE BASIC GAME: BLOCK DOMINOES

This is the equivalent to the '301 standard game' in darts. The aim is to be the first person to get rid of all the dominoes. With 2 players, each take seven tiles; 3 or 4 players take either five or six of the blocks. The other dominoes are left aside in what is usually called the 'Boneyard'. Normally, if convention matters, this drawing of dominoes from the face-down assortment on the table is done in rotation. The person who has drawn the 'heaviest' domino prior to the start of the game starts proceedings by laying a domino on the table. (In some areas the starting domino will be the highest double in anyone's hand. This rather than a previous draw would then determine the person to commence.) In doubles play this will indicate to the partner which suit (i.e. numbers) may be preferred.

Play continues around the table until a player can't go. He or she indicates this by 'knocking' the table. All doubles are played across the line of dominoes and not lengthways:

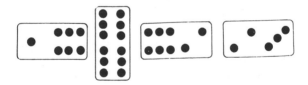

In most games someone will manage to get rid of all their dominoes. Where this doesn't occur, play ends when all the players can't go. The total of the 'pips' on the players' tiles are totalled up at the end of the round. Either the person who goes out first or the person with the lowest score left in their hand wins the round. Play continues for an agreed number of rounds.

A VARIATION ON THE THEME

This game is exactly the same except that players may put on the table as many tiles as they wish in each go, as long as they join by numbers. So, the person commencing might lay down five dominoes, leaving only one. Player 2, could then put down only two and Player 3 is blocked by Player 2 'closing-off' each end with the same number.

A hint which is useful for all new players is that they should try to get rid of all their 'heavy' tiles first, thereby avoiding the risks of being caught with a high score.

With both the traditional games, we found that they worked best with younger children under twelve and were better in the singles versions, rather than in pairs. At least a few squabbles were avoided.

In pairs' games there are a couple of other rules:
>   (1) The winner of the previous hand starts.
>   (2) Pairs score jointly; as soon as one of the pair is out they score all the pips left. Some domino games are played where both partners must get out for their side to win.

The game **can** catch the imagination of youngsters, or at least their liking for the mundane and repetitive. At other times it may be best to pass immediately on to what we view as a more interesting game before putting the kids off the use of dominoes.

DRAW DOMINOES

This variation of the game is the same as in the standard block game, excepting that fewer tiles are drawn at the start of the game. So, for instance, each player might only have five 'tiles' each. When a person is blocked they then draw from the pool of the 'boneyard'. This style of playing can be 'attached' to almost any of the games, usually ensuring that a conclusion of someone going out is reached.

FIVES AND THREES

Requiring a wee bit of brain-work, this game offers more variety for players and was a firm favourite with some of our groups of young people. It is a combination of 3 other games, known as Muggins, All-fives and All-threes. With 2, 3 or 4 players, each draws 6 tiles.

A player leads with any domino - but the aim is to place tiles which add up to a number divisible by 3 or 5, or even both, like 15. For instance, if the first player puts down a double six, they score $12 \div 3 = 4$ points. In the example below the second player makes a total of 15, double-six plus a three at the other end of the line. This gives that player a score of 8; $15 \div 3 = 5$ and $15 \div 5 = 3$; $5 + 3 = 8$. A cribbage board is useful for scoring, marking up the points as they are gained.

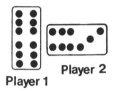

Player 2

Player 1

The game is played up to 31 or 61 and the exact number must be achieved. This will probably take 3 or 4 hands - about the right length of play for youngsters. The partnership game can be played, as with the standard game, either by having one or both players using up all their tiles. Singles play ends, obviously, when a player uses the last block, or when everyone cannot go.

ST. ANDREW'S CROSS

Could this be Scottish? Well, we tried for a touch of 'north of the border', didn't we? With 4 players, this game is based on a double-four lead. Each player draws six tiles until someone can play this double-four lead. There are only 4 'sleepers' in the boneyard, so it shouldn't take too long. As can be seen in the diagram, each player has their 'own' line, lettered A, E, C, & D.

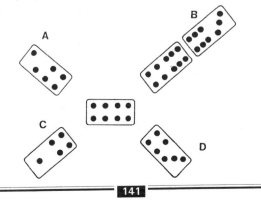

Play proceeds in the normal way, one tile being played by each player, but only on their own line. If a player is 'blocked' and knocks, the next player in sequence can play on the blocked players' line and their own, thus getting rid of two dominoes in a turn. The game ends when a player goes out or the game is blocked so no-one can go. Spots are totalled etc.

BERGEN

We found that this was fun, challenging and rewarding. It is a combination of the essence of various other games. The aim is for the 2, 3 or 4 players to be the first out, but there is also a strong element of blocking - making it a very assertive game. If a player can make the two ends have the same number they score 2 points. Playing a double to make both ends the same, scores 3 points. Playing against a double also gives 3 points. By this we mean, adding a new block onto a double which gives the same number as at the other end i.e.

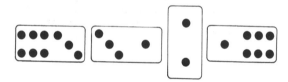

Placing the 1 and 6 gives a 3 score.

The start of the game is with 6 dominoes for 2 or 3 players and 5 tiles for 4 players. The highest double starts and players unable or unwilling to add to the sequence must draw from the boneyard. A player getting rid of their final domino also scores 2 points. Game score is normally 15.

Altogether it is different enough to appeal to newcomers and old-hands at the game.

BLIND HUGHIE

One supposes that any section should have an idiotic, 'silly' game. This is it! It is also Scottish, originating with 'slightly' worse for wear Fife miners. Between 2 and 5 maniacs are required and each draws 5 blocks. No player looks at the blocks and all are lined up face down in front of the individuals concerned. Player One turns over the block on the left of the line and places it in the centre of the table. Player Two turns over his similar domino and if it matches block 1, it is played in the normal way. If it doesn't it is placed, face upwards at the right hand end of the player's line of blocks.

It all helps to get the dominoes back into their box at the end of the session !

POOL

In Britain, pool has 'taken over' from the traditional games of snooker, billiards and bar-billiards. The species of pool played almost universally is so standard as not to be worth repeating. It is best known as 'eight ball pool' because the black 8 ball is the last to be pocketed, each player or team potting either spots (solid coloured balls) or stripes and then pot black. The only variations which may add to the games which you play with youth groups are concerning the end game, i.e. potting the black. Regrettably, the full game of pool cannot be played on most tables because they have 'sealed' pockets and have different markings.

End Games:

1) In the standard game players nominate which pocket the black ball is aimed for and that player is only the winner if the ball is successfully potted in that pocket.

2) An 'alternative' and easier end game is simply potting the black without nomination.

3) 'Last Bag'. This one is more fun and skilful. Whichever pocket a player's ball goes in becomes 'their pocket' for the black. If the game is level, this can make for an exciting and frustrating chase of cat and dog up and down the table. Players may not have the same pocket and if this does occur the second player's home-base is the one opposite, either diagonally or horizontally.

4) Much the same as in version 3, but it is the first ball into the pocket from each player that establishes the pocket for the end game. A useful tip to aid a decaying memory is to put a 'marker' by the respective pockets.

5) Potting the black ball can be made much more nerve-racking by stipulating that since both players are 'on the black', a foul stroke loses the game.

A source of some disagreement in all the pool-style games concerns whether an 'extra shot' given after a foul stroke is 'carried on'. By this, we mean, if Player A miscues and misses all the balls, pots an opponent's ball or strikes a ball off the table, 2 strokes are allowed for Player B. In question is what happens if Player B pots a ball, do they still have 2 strokes? Some say yes, some no. We sit on the fence, but it is worthwhile knowing in advance that you may be required to adjudicate!

Pool doesn't much lend itself to alternative games, not at least of a type that a youth worker would want to encourage. We offer just a few alternatives:

ROTATION

The balls are set out as in the diagram:

Players both start by aiming at the ball numbered No. 1.

They are trying to pot it, or hit the 1 ball and rebound it or the cue ball on to a higher value ball striking it into a pocket i.e.

THE REBOUND SHOT

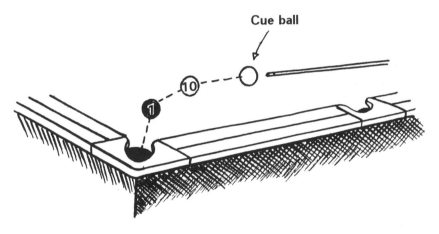

Cue ball

It's a sort of combination of pool and billiards. Scoring is achieved by potting the balls, either in strict order - rotation 1, 2, 3, 4, etc. or by rebound shots, which obviously allow for rapid scoring. A successful 'pot' gives the player an additional shot, as with most other games of this type. We used a two shot penalty or a 2 point penalty for foul shots: i.e.

    (1) missing all the balls
    (2) hitting a wrong ball
    (3) potting a wrong ball

The winner is the player with the highest score, when all the balls have disappeared (preferably inside the machine!).

POOL GOLF

This game cannot be played on a pool table unless the coin mechanism is set to automatically return the balls. The first player selects one ball to act as club and one as ball for a 'round' of golf. Each player has their own club and their own ball for the duration of the game - an easy(ish) way to remember whose ball belongs to which player is to arrange it so that 'spots' are the golf balls and 'stripes' the clubs. If these are paired off according to colour, they are readily identifiable.

The golf ball is placed on the top of table spot and the club in the 'D'. A 1st hole is chosen and that is the target. The cue is used to hit the club ball towards the respective golf ball. Each player proceeds in this way, one stroke at a time and scoring a particular number of shots per hole en route. This continues with each player shooting in turn until a ball is potted, then that player goes again for the next hole, playing clockwise around the table. Each pocket represents a hole, and once around the table represents a six-hole golf competition. If you don't want to remember how many strokes have been taken, the game can be played with the first person to finish (as in pool) being declared the winner.

Penalties

When a player pots either of their balls by mistake this gives a penalty of 'losing one hole' and that player shoots again for the previous pocket. When a player pots an opposing player's ball, they return to the previous hole.

Missing your own ball did not incur any penalty in the version we played, nor did hitting an opponent's ball without potting it. Overall, it's quite a popular game as long as there are not more than three players. Two is better since the pace of the game is increased.

RACING

Ideally for this game, you need a pool table where you will not have to pay.

It's a 'one-at-a-time' game, each person playing against the clock. One ball, it doesn't matter what colour or value, is placed on the spot at the top of the table and the white cue ball is placed in the D. The player tries to pot the ball at the top of the table. Whether this effort is successful or otherwise, the result is the same. Another ball is brought up as a new cue ball, again regardless of what it is. Within a two minute period or whatever limit is set, the player scores one point for each ball potted. Once you have run out of 'cue balls', you have to stop even if you are still within the time limit. Any number can compete and it allows plenty of opportunity for kids to try out their new digital watches with the timer function. It's wild and fun, but take care not to get the cloth ripped!

At the end of a round, the player with the highest score wins.

SIDES

Played as in the standard 8-ball game, with one side taking spots and the other, stripes, there is an extra difference indicated by which side of the table the first ball goes down. That side is then the player's personal domain and all that player's balls must be potted in the 3 pockets along that side. Failure to do so, incurs the standard 2 stroke penalty. The black ball end game can be played in a number of ways, but normally the black must be potted in one of the pockets nominated on the player's side of the table.

A good game to vary the monotony and one which requires an extra degree of skill - so it should preferably be introduced with youngsters who have mastered the standard game.

CARD GAMES

There are literally thousands of games using a pack or packs of cards. We are not intending even the slightest attempt at comprehensive coverage. Instead we have selected games which youngsters have subjected us to with surprisingly pleasing results and games with which we have returned the compliment.

Games with cards fall into two distinct categories for our purposes and then those games may be further sub-divided. Some are primarily games of chance; others rely on a range of skills:

memory, careful timing and/or good partnership. We were surprised how many of the kids we played with were not used to even 'standard' games such as Knockout Whist. That one we include, whilst most of the others in this section are 'fun' games aimed at involvement rather than sorting out potential Einsteins. Many are quite noisy, so don't go thinking that card games are automatically destined for the quiet room! We hope that you find a few gems which you can use with the young people you know, or are working with. There aren't many games included which are going to reduce the loose change in your pocket!

SWITCH

A highly ritualised version of this was introduced to us by a group of extrovert girls in a youth club. It is a game largely of chance and a round can last some time - but it's fun and is distinctly odd!

Each player is dealt seven cards. The top card is turned over, and the player to the left of the dealer has a range of choices. A player may:
1) Follow suit (i.e. club on club).
2) Follow number (i.e. 5 on 5).
3) Play an ace, which can be played anytime and allows the player to choose a new suit.

Other cards have peculiar powers as well.
A **QUEEN** reverses the order of play and allows the player to put down an additional card, (i.e. left or right direction). Playing a **TWO** means that the next player must pick up two cards from the pack and miss a go (**another TWO** may be played by the following

player. in which case four cards must be picked up by the next player, and so on). A **SIX** is the really weird card! This leads to a **SWITCH**, not of direction but of total hand i.e. a six is played and everyone must pass on all their cards to the next person in the direction of play. Players who cannot go, pick up one card.

When there is only one card left in a player's hand they must announce the fact. Failure brings a penalty of one pick-up card. Very annoying to the recipient. The winner is the first person to get rid of all the cards. Altogether quite entertaining - and distinctly odd!

GO FISHING

"Lively and different", as they say in all promotional blurbs. 'Go Fishing' we have played with groups of up to 5 players. In these cases, each individual is dealt 9 cards. For more than 5, only 8 or even 7 cards are distributed, otherwise there will not be any pack for 'pick-ups'.

The Dealer starts and play continues in a clockwise direction. In a turn, Player A asks any other individual for cards of a certain value, say, for instance, a player has at least one six they may ask Player C for sixes and receive two. A player may only ask for cards of any value, if they hold at least one of the type in their hand. But, when they are successful in obtaining, say, sixes from a player, they may then: (a) ask the same player for cards of another value or (b) ask another player for some particular cards.

When asked, a player must hand over all the cards of a particular value. A turn ends when a player has failed to 'find' the card/cards which they are seeking. The player then picks up the top card from the pack. If this card is of the same denomination as the one asked for, the player continues. When a player fails to find the cards sought, the turn ends and a card is picked up. Play then moves on to the turn of the next player in a clockwise direction.

The aim is to make sets of 4 which are immediately put down on the table. Any set of 4 cards scores 40 points, except aces, which score 60 points. If a player runs out of cards, he or she must pick up a card from the pack; if no cards are left then that player totals up their score and drops out of the game.

The game ends when every set is on the table. The person with the most points at the end wins, or in the case of a draw, players enter into a novel end game of a **TIEBREAK**, which is:
The players involved shuffle the pack and a cut is made. Then each player in turn takes the top card and this continues until one draws an ace. That player is the eventual winner.

KNOCKOUT WHIST
The most common of the games we have included. It is still a proven success. It can be played with between 3 and 7 players. With any number of players, 7 cards are dealt to each and the top card of the remainder is turned over. For the first hand this dictates the Trump suit.

The player to the dealer's left leads and other players follow suit if they can, or trump or discard to the lead if they don't have any cards of the correct suit. Tricks are kept by individual players and the highest number of tricks won allows that player to choose trumps in the next hand. After the round with 7 cards, the sequence is repeated with 6 cards and then 5 and so on down to 1. If any player fails to win a trick they then receive 1 card in the following hand which they can play at any time during that hand. If they win a trick they are back in the game. For obvious reasons, this extra 'life' does not take place after the two or one card hands! Players who have failed to make a 'trick' in these hands are well and truly 'knocked out'.

ROCKAWAY

This combines fun and lunacy with some level of skill. It's easy enough to learn, yet reasonably satisfying for all the players. Any number can play and almost any age group. Seven cards are dealt to each player face downwards and one card is placed face upwards in the centre of the table - this is known as the 'Kitty'. All discards are placed onto this kitty throughout the game.

The aim is to be the first player to get rid of all the cards in the hand. This is done simply by discarding onto the kitty, following either:

> *THE SUIT (i.e. diamonds) THE NUMBER (i.e. 5) or PLAYING AN ACE (which are wild and can only be followed by another ace or a card of the same suit).*

Skill is shown in careful planning of the discards. An ace should not be played unless necessary. If a player cannot go, they must draw from the remainder of the pack, which has been placed face downwards on the table. After the pack runs out, players miss a turn only if they cannot go.

The winner plays his or her last card onto the discard and then the score is totalled up as a negative score against other individuals:

> *ACE scores:15; COURT cards:10; OTHER CARDS face value.*

It's quite fun, reasonably active and not too hard to supervise.

BLACKOUT

Simplicity itself, Blackout is played with between 3 and 7 players. The aim, as in whist, is to win tricks AND accurately predict the right number of tricks. Some cards are discarded from the pack, but not exposed, depending on the number of players.

	Tricks
With 3 players 1 card is left out	17
With 4 the whole pack is used	13
With 5 players 2 cards are left out	10
With 6 players 4 cards are left out	8
With 7 players 3 cards are left out	7

The whole pack is dealt out, with the last card to the dealer's hand being exposed - this is then the **TRUMP SUIT**. The person on the dealer's left now says how many tricks they hope to make and this continues around the table. Say, with 4 players, these calls might be: (out of a possible 13 tricks)

PLAYER A	7
PLAYER B	4
PLAYER C	2
PLAYER D	2
Total	= 15

The last player to bid **must not** make a bid which, taken together with the other bids adds up to the correct number of tricks for the game. Play then commences, as in whist. The player to the left of the dealer leads and when that 'trick' has been won, the winner leads.

Suits led must be followed if possible, otherwise they can be trumped or cards can be 'thrown'. At the end of a round the tricks are scored at 1 point each, with 10 point bonuses for any players making the number they originally bid. A total of 50 or a 100 points can herald the end of the game. A competitive and clever game, slightly akin to Bridge.

MINORU or THE DERBY

If spending lunchtimes in the Betting Office is your youth group's favourite pastime, this is the ideal game. You need some counters since the game simulates a horse race and the gambling which precedes it. First mark out a large sheet of paper, as follows:

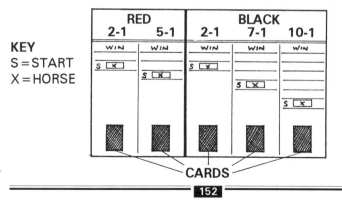

Players then place their stakes, i.e. counters, above the columns and the person acting as banker keeps an eye on proceedings.

The race starts: 5 cards are dealt, face downwards onto the spaces at the bottom of the columns. These are the 'horses'. Below these, five cards are dealt face upwards. The horse with the highest card gets a move one column up the course. The race continues with cards being dealt until a horse reaches the top line which is the finishing post.

The odds are correct mathematically, with a slight advantage for the banker. We suggest that each player takes 4 turns as banker before passing on the bank. Players may also bet on 'red' or 'black' - the banker pays even money.

SPOONS

Our name for a furious, noise-filled bit of nonsense, which is a card party game. It's ideal with young groups, or a wide age-range. The slightly 'special' equipment required is spoons, one less in number than the players, and an old pack of cards from which sets of 4 (of a kind, kings or aces for example) are extracted. The number of sets corresponds with the number of participants.

The spoons are placed in the centre of the table at the beginning of the game. Play involves shuffling the sets of cards, dealing 4 cards to each player, after which each player chooses a card from his or her hand to pass onto the person on the left. All the cards are passed, at the same time, face down. The new cards are looked at, a new 'pass-on' is chosen and all the players make another change of hand. As soon as one player has a set of 4 cards they should quietly put them face upwards on the table, shout 'spoons!' and grab a spoon. Other players have to pay some attention, for they must also reach for spoons at this point. The loser is the one left 'spoonless'. Various means are used to score the game, but it is normally negative-scoring i.e. the first person to lose 6 games may have to perform a forfeit.

It is the sort of game, which, if used in a session of 'heavier' and 'lighter' experiences is an excellent tension breaker.

SEQUENCE

Groups of 4 or 5 are best for this game, but 2 or more can play. The aim is to get rid of cards before the opponents. All the cards are dealt out between the players. The player on the dealer's left puts down on the table the lowest card (2's count lowest; ace high) in their hand and the player with the next card must follow the sequence i.e. the 2 of hearts would be followed by the 3 of the same suit.The sequence continues until the ace is played. At this point the player of the ace plays any card of their choice. The sequence continues until the ace is reached, or where a suit has been used before up to the highest card left to be played. The next sequence is then started by the person who played the last card.The winner is the person to play all their cards first.

If more than one round is required, then a scoring system can be devised, say for instance, the first player to win 3 rounds is the overall champion of Sequence. The playing of the sequence 'starter' cards is quite skilful and staff won't mind participating too much. We found that this game was rather contagious and we were still suffering outbreaks weeks after the game was introduced.

SHOVE HA'PENNY

An English contrivance first used in pubs. It can be made of wood or slate, and the size, if you were thinking of making your own is

2 ft long by 1 ft 2" wide with the grain running lengthwise. Often the top end of the board has a semi-circular raised edge to prevent the ha'pennies going over the top end. Ten lines (grooves) in the board run horizontally across the table and each of the nine beds are one and a quarter inch wide. Squares on each side of the beds, divided by a vertical groove provide space for chalking in each player's score. This is normally done by marking two horizontal lines: '**II**', and then when the player's bed is full a third line strikes through thus: '**H**'.

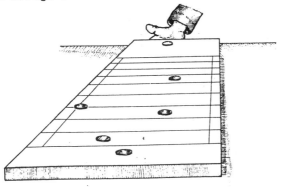

The game has limited appeal with youth groups but can be a valued piece of equipment if used intelligently. However, it is unlikely to compete for popularity with the pool table. Each player has five discs to 'shove' up the board with palm of hand, thumb or tips of fingers-all are legal. The aim is to get three ha'pennies in each of the nine beds. Coins overlapping the lines in any way are adjudged 'out'. Normally coins which cross the first line are in play, otherwise if the ha'penny is mis-hit and **hasn't** hit another coin or touched the first line, they can be taken back to the beginning of the board and restruck. Once a player has 3 in a bed it is viewed as full for that player, and if that player shoves another coin into the bed, and the opponent has not filled up the bed, then that other player receives a bonus 'credit' - one point for each coin so misplaced.

The winner is the first player to fill every bed. A game can last over half an hour, so some youngsters may get rather bored. Reducing the 'full-bed' size to two or one is one way around the difficulty.

PROGRESSIVE SHOVE HA'PENNY

Like the standard game, 'Progressive' is played on the specially made board. It is more suitable for experienced players, so cannot really be used as an alternative for beginners.

The difference from the standard game is a minor one, but it changes the nature of play. 'Scoring' coins can be taken back and re-struck, thus a skilful player may score many of the 27 bedplaces before the opponent gets a go.

31

Requiring a marking system for the board, the beds score 1-9 points. '1 ' is nearest the strike end of the board. The aim is to score exactly 31 points, although any other target score can be chosen. Once a player is at 25, they must score exactly 6 to finish. A score of 7 would 'bust' and they return to the last number. Quite fun, we found with beginners.

JACKS AND FIVESTONES

Athough these are commonly regarded as Primary School playground games, we were nicely surprised (for a change) when they created a real craze and waves of nostalgia amongst a group of 14 year olds. Unusual in this collection, it is not purely competitive, since the 'practising' solo, takes as much time as the game. The objective is to complete a series of increasingly difficult throws with either the small coloured cubes called fivestones, or the jacks, which are small metal or plastic 6-legged objects, usually supplied in sets of five or six.

We include here the basic game and a few variants. Even if you don't find any fives fans, at least having the equipment at hand won't cost you the earth!

FIVESTONES

The Basic Game: The basic throw involves tossing the stones from the palm of the hand and catching them on the back of the hand. The process is then reversed and the stones on the back of the hand are tossed and caught in the palm. Ones and Twos are games linked to the basic throw. In **Ones**, the player makes the basic throw. If all are dropped the turn ends. If one or more are caught, the dropped stones are left on the ground while the player moves all but one of the stones caught to the other hand. The single stone is thrown up and the player picks up or attempts to pick up one stone from the ground then catches the airborne item. This is all completed with the one hand. The procedure is repeated until all the stones have been retrieved.

If successful, the player goes on to **Twos**. The second player would, on their turn go through the same process.

Twos is played by scattering the stones on the ground not too far apart. One piece is selected and this is tossed, while two pieces are picked up from the ground in the same hand. Success leads to repeating the process with the remaining two stones. Threes and Fours are the same as Twos but with a larger 'pick-up'.

Another variation is a sequence known as **PECKS, BUSHELS, AND CLAWS**. In **Pecks,** the basic throw is attempted. If successful the player moves on to **Bushels**. A catch of one or more, then involves the turnover. Holding the caught stones in the throwing hand, one stone is pushed between forefinger and thumb. This is thrown in the air while that hand is used to pick up one stone at a time from the ground, until all have been retrieved and the player attempts Bushels. In this, the basic throw again begins the sequence, success immediately moves the thrower onto an attempt at **Claws**. Bushels involves throwing up in the air all the stones caught and picking up one stone from the ground in the interim. This is repeated until all the grounded stones are in hand.

Claws starts with the basic throw and if successful moves onto the ones, twos sequence. Dropping any (not all, which would end the player's turn) leads to placing all the caught stones on the back of the hand and picking up the remaining stones between each of the fingers and/finger and thumb, one to each gap. Once in position, the stones on the back of the hand are thrown and caught in the palm. Then the between-finger stones are manoeuvred from their position to the palm, completing the sequence.

JACKS

These are usually used in conjunction with a ball (small rubber type), though not necessarily so. The ball is bounced or thrown up and caught in the second hand while the sequence with the jacks is taking place in the other hand.

Over the Jump is a popular jacks game, not using the ball. The non throwing hand is placed palm downwards and 4 jacks are situated to one side of the hand. One jack is thrown in the air either from the back or palm of the hand (you decide the rule at the outset) and while the thrown piece is in the air, one jack at a time is transferred from one side of the hand (jump) to the other. Once all 4 are over the jump, the player throws the first jack and must make a pickup of 4. That ends the sequence.

As with many of the games listed, if you as an adult show that you are willing to get involved and play at a shared level, jacks can work in the most unlikely of child and adolescent situations, AND we'd point out that it's not a girls' game!

MARBLE GAMES

We thought that it was strange that it took us from 1979 right through to 1994 to find a place for 'Marbles' in the Games Book. But it's here now, and we have had some fun trying out some of the half-forgotten forms of the game.

Thinking back to our own childhood days of playing marbles, the game was simple. One person would roll their glass marble along the ground, often using the gutter of the road or the pavement as the playing arena. Then, the other player would try and hit the first marble with their own. Taking alternate turns, the game would continue until one person managed to hit the other's marble. This hit would win the loser's marble. This version of marbles is commonly called **'Capture'**. The only main variation was when one player had a 'special' marble, which was either larger, more ornate, or a ball-bearing. These special marbles would be classified as 'two-ers' or 'three-ers', which meant that they had to be hit more times before they could be won and change ownership. Historically, marbles were also made of wood, stone and plastic.

Marble games tend to be played avidly as 'craze' by kids. For a time it becomes an all consuming passion, which, like most other passions, subsides after a while. For youth workers or parents, it is a simple game to introduce, popular, and requires little equipment or expense. Very nicely made, traditional marbles, can be cheaply purchased at many toy and gift shops. Many of these are often referred to as 'alleys' because of the flecks of colour which swirl through the white or clear glass, rather like the colours which flow through a person's eye.

Finally, before moving on to describing some of the games you can play with marbles, a quick word about the ways in which you can **'shoot' or roll** your marbles. We know of three ways of propelling the marble on its way:

1) The simplest is just to hold the marble in one hand and roll it in the required direction.

2) Shooting requires more dexterity. The marble is held as in the

drawing below, with the player's knuckles placed firmly on the ground. The marble is shot forward by a flick of the thumb. This technique is sometimes called 'knuckling'.

3) A third method is simply to flick the marble from its position on the ground with the thumb.

But, on to some of the games variations.......................

SPANNING

This is played the same way as 'Capture' but with one significant rule change. Either player can elect to 'span' the two marbles if they are close enough together. Spanning is undertaken by a player placing their thumb on their own marble and a finger on the opponent's marble, and then flicking them together. If a span is successful, the 'spanner' captures the opponent's marble; if unsuccessful, the player loses their own marble.

RING O' MARBLES

Two circles must be drawn on the ground to play this game. We have used chalk on the pavement and we have also played it on a sandy beach. The inner circle is about a foot in diameter, the outer circle approximately 6 or 7 feet. Any small number of players can participate, with each putting two of their marbles into the inner circle.

Each player takes it in turns to shoot from any point outside of the outer circle. Their aim is to knock marbles out of the inner circle. In different versions of the game, they then either win these displaced marbles or get an extra shot.
Each succeeding shot is taken from where the player's marble last came to rest. Another twist in the game is to allow players to also

also shoot at their opponents' marbles, and if they hit them they are captured. An additional rule makes any marble that comes to rest in the inner circle a target. That player then starts with a new marble from outside of the big circle. Play continues until all the marbles have been removed from the inner circle.

WALL MARBLES

As you've guessed from the name, this game requires a wall!

Players take turns to roll their marbles towards the wall so that they hit the wall and rebound back towards the players. Each player then takes their turn with the aim of hitting opponents' marbles on the rebound, in which case **all** of the marbles played are captured. After the first round of play, players shoot their marbles from the position where they first landed. In different versions of the game, the marbles may either still be required to hit and rebound off the wall or may be played as in capture. In the latter version of the game, only one marble at a time can be captured after the first round.

BOMBS AWAY

This game is different. A small circle is marked on the ground and each player puts one or more marbles into the circle. They then take turns to stand above the circle and carefully drop a marble down onto the circle. The aim is to knock marbles out of the circle, which they then capture. If a marble is knocked out of the circle, the successful player also keeps their original marble; if they fail, they must add the marble they have dropped, into the circle.

TARGETS

There are numerous target games which can be played using marbles, and it is fun to improvise your own. Most can be played indoors or out of doors. Ideas for such games include:

1) Line up an agreed number of marbles with at least two marble's space between them (say, one from each player.) This line should be at least six feet away from the shooting line. Players then take turns to shoot at the **marble line**. Any marbles hit are captured,

and a hit gives the player an extra shot.

2) **Toy soldiers, lego figures, or similar** can also be used for targets in a target game, and it can be fun to place obstacles in the line of fire to deflect the oncoming marbles. Knocking over a figure scores an agreed number of points.

3) An **archboard** can be constructed, or bought, which provides a target for a marble scoring game. Such a board can be made of wood or stiff cardboard. Players can either roll alternate marbles and keep their scores as they go, or roll up five or ten marbles as a 'go'. The winner is the person with the highest score at the end of an agreed number of rounds.

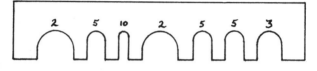

4) **'Hundreds'** is quite a popular game and easy to organise. A playing area of about 6-10 feet is agreed and a circle is drawn or small hole dug for a target area. Players then take turns to try and roll their marbles into the target. Each successful marble scores ten points and gives the player an additional turn. A miss doesn't score and play moves on to the next player.

Notes.

Section Six:
ACTIVITY GAMES

INTRODUCTION

The fact that this section is slimmer than its counterparts bears no real reflection on how we view activity games. We do not see them having lower priority than two player games or relationship exercises. That leads us to a large BUT. Activity games in the recent past, and especially in America have suddenly become big business. Big business, that is, in the nicest sense of the phrase. Co-operative games and New Games have spawned a batch of publications and like some latter day Pied Pipers, Andrew Fleugelman, Stewart Brand, Terry Orlick and friends have been staging one day festivals of games attracting hundreds of participants. All these have been aimed at demonstrating the advantages of physical trust and·fun over aggressiveness and competitive sport. The approach has won over a large number of converts and 'New Games' initiatives, events and 'one-offs' are currently taking place around Britain, with workers in social work, community education and youth work heading the experiment.

We tried out a few of the games from this new source and in this section we offer these and some more traditional team games as examples of what to do with a larger group of youngsters in a gym hall or in the great outside! There is no attempt on our part either to duplicate the content of the 'New Games Book' or the 'Co-operative Sports and Games Book' or to enter the Sports arena, whereby we would find ourselves describing football, tennis and rugby. Instead, we recommend you to beg, borrow or the other thing - a copy of the New Games Book, and along with marvelling at its outstanding level of production, enjoy the games described.

Finally in this section, we mention three games which are commercially marketed products. Uni-hoc, Frisbee, and Swing-ball are all in use in the centres we visited. They work well, and **as resources** they should be considered. Once tried on a couple of occasions the response can be assessed and where a piece of equipment is obviously successful then that can act as the focus for fund-raising activity on the part of the youth group. Along our route as games book compilers we found ourselves saving pennies for a second-hand pool table and a set of Uni-hoc!

FREEZE TAG

Designate a quarter of your group 'IT' and they can then attempt to touch - 'freeze' the rest of the group. When touched a person must stop in the position where they have been tagged. Up until this point the game sounds rather normal and tedious, but there is a catch. All those people who haven't been tagged yet can 'unfreeze' those who have been tagged, so the inevitable result is a hall full of statues who spring to life with alarming vigour! Normally those who are 'IT' yell 'FREEZE' when touching a captive and the players who have not been tagged call 'UNFREEZE' when freeing the captives.

TUNNEL TIG

Exactly the same as FREEZE TAG, but with about 5 people 'IT' to begin with. When a person is frozen they stand with legs apart. Players who have not been 'tigged' can unfreeze them by crawling through the legs. An absolutely exhausting game, but an enjoyable one. We found it useful for part of an evening session - perhaps for twenty minutes or so.

CHAIN-GANG

This version of tag turned up in the New Games Book as the Blob. We enjoyed it in the school playground and it seemed to go down well in the youth club hall.

One person is 'IT', and they try to tag another person. Once this happens they join hands and continue on the rampage. The chain becomes longer as the number of 'free' players is reduced. The chain gang can itself split up, as long as at least two people are joined together. This normally speeds up the catching process, but perhaps it reduces the fun, since a long, twisting chain gang is much more of a co-operative venture. The game finishes, or at least that round, when no more free players exist.

VAMPIRE

The New Games people obviously went to Transylvania for this game. All the participants close their eyes and mill amongst all the other warm-blooded bodies of their erstwhile neighbours. The referee quietly tells one 'miller' that he or she is the vampire. They still keep eyes closed but as soon as the vampire bumps into another person they grab them (no bites, please!) and let out a suitably authentic blood-curdling scream. Victims become vampires and they prowl for new victims. If that was it, there would soon be a shortage of new blood, **but** when a vampire grabs another vampire they both revert to human form!

CATERPILLAR

This is another New Game. Everyone should be lying on their stomachs, side by side. The people should be sardine-like, very closely packed together. The person at one end then rolls all the way across the top of the bodies, the next person from that end following along close behind. Once the rhythm gets going the Caterpillar will make quite some speed across a hall floor or field. An obvious extension of the idea is to have caterpillar races. For each caterpillar you need at least ten people to make it worthwhile.

EGG TOSS

This is typical of the 'play hard, play fair, nobody hurt' New Games philosophy. Competition is allowed and encouraged as long as it's fun, but more important is the overriding ethic that losing is fun. (Usually this game is played with small water filled balloons, rather than eggs).

Played out of doors, all the players are lined up in pairs facing one another in two long lines. Each pair have their own balloon and on the instruction they throw the water-balloon across the four to five foot gap. After each round, the partners move another foot apart. When balloons burst or are dropped that pair drop out. The last two left win and are usually invited to do as they will with their wet missile!

DODGE BALL

As with many evolving games there can be numerous versions of a game, under various guises. Dodge Ball is a good example. Here are two adaptations of the game which we have played with mixed age groups (12-18). With a bit of supervision to prevent outright bloodshed it provides an ideal opportunity to let off steam.

Version 1
All the players assemble in the playing area. We tried it with over 40 in a slightly larger than standard badminton hall. One person has the ball and throws it at any other player, aiming at the legs, below the kneecaps. Players may 'dodge' or fist the ball away. Any player may then pick up the ball and project it at the other participants, again aiming at the lower leg area. Any players hit **must** leave the playing area. The game continues (with upwards of 30, for twenty minutes or so) until there is a winner i.e. only one person left on court.

Version 2
Players are divided into two equal groups. One group forms a large circle - the others become the 'dodgers', inside the circle. Play for 6 to 8 minutes with about 15 a side. The aim is for the circle players to pass the ball around and then throw it at those inside. A hit on **any part** of the body counts and that player must retire from the circle.

No 'circle' player may enter the circle, except to retrieve the ball, in which case they must pass it to one of their circle formation. After the time period is up, the number of 'hit' players are counted and this forms the basis for comparison, as the teams switch around.

BATTLE BALL

Despite the openly aggressive title of the game, there is virtually no physical contact between players. Two teams of 5 play one another for a fixed time, say five minutes, or until all the skittles are knocked over. The playing area is divided up as below:

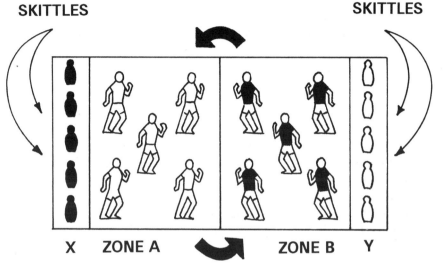

SKITTLES   SKITTLES

X   ZONE A   ZONE B   Y

No player from zone A may enter B or vice versa. Areas marked in the diagram 'X' and 'Y' are also out of bounds except for retrieval purposes. The aim is for each side to pass the ball between their players and then to aim at the skittles (which are at least three feet apart at each end of the hall).

The ball may be intercepted and it can be lobbed or rolled. For variety, the game can be played using 2 or more balls. As a comment, we found the game very successful with 14+ and good with mixed sex groups, since, although the ball tends to be thrown with some force by aggressive male characters, the gentle, accurate lob may prove more successful in decimating the opposition skittles.

CORNER GOAL BALL

With a pitch divided as below, mark out 4 corner 'goal' areas before starting to play. As with Battle Ball, each team must stay in their own half, but instead of trying to knock down skittles, the aim is to pass the ball to either of the corner goals in the opponent's half. Each time the ball reaches the corner goal it counts as a goal, and during an agreed time period both teams try to score as often as possible.

A rule which we tried and seems to work with teenage groups is to allow the goalkeepers to move around outside the goal area as long as they keep one foot in their area. However, a goal can only be scored by placing the ball down in the corner goal. As with battle-ball, players can pass between themselves and try to intercept shots at goal. One interesting aspect of the game, is that **after** a goal the goalkeeper must try to throw the ball back to his own team which is not always easy!

UNIHOC

(Imported by C. G. Davies and Son, Coventry)
Is it a commercial game or do we remember playing Indoor Hockey with socks wrapped around walking sticks? Anyway, this is the name of the new commercial version, and for once it is a game which lives up to the claims made in the publicity handouts. The sticks are manufactured in Sweden and are made from strong, flexible polyethylene plastic which is light enough for even young players. An added advantage is that neither the coloured sticks nor the air-ball/puck which is used for the game mark the floor. Even the house-proud manager of our new local Community Centre wore a wide smile of contentment at the end of our hour-long sessions.

The game itself is fast and tiring and the number of players per side can be varied to suit the size of the hall or outdoor area. In using Unihoc for more than a dozen sessions, we were delighted with the high level of involvement and anticipation which was evident in every game. Mixed sex groups and an age range of 12-17 can easily be accommodated in the same arena, as the skill and ball control inherent in hockey overcomes the basic instinct

for physical aggression. In all then, a valuable asset and not too expensive. It would seem to us to be a wise investment either for individual clubs and centres or for an area worker to take around to clubs on a 'game-tasting' basis. The same firm (C. G. Davies) also market 'UNI-TENNIS', which is a good value for money version of indoor tennis using plastic rackets and sponge balls. It's a successfully interchangeable game, useful as a fun interlude or as a competitive sport.

FRISBEE
(Manufacturer: The Frisbee Co. Ltd.)
Frisbee is a new game in itself and probably most families now own at least one. Here are three outdoor games which you might enjoy trying. We found that they were useful in working up a thirst!

FRISBEE GOLF
Two, three or four players bring along their favourite frisbees to a nice large open space or park. There, the first hole is agreed upon. An object, maybe two hundred yards away is the hole and in turn

each player tries to reach the hole (hitting the object) in the fewest possible strokes (throws). After the first hole a new hole is chosen and each player in turn again throws for the new target. A score for the round is kept.

THROW AND RUN

While the golf game is relatively gentle, this game we developed is the opposite. The course is much the same as for 'golf'. 200 yards with a tee and a target is all you need, though we found that an ideal target might be a football goal or a sizeable tree. The thrower stands at the tee and the other player or players position themselves between the thrower and the target at a distance they would expect the frisbee to travel through the air. The thrower now launches the frisbee and the other participants try to catch the flying disc. If any of them is successful they can throw the frisbee anywhere (within the bounds of the field) they like. The thrower now scores the number of throws it takes them to reach the target, i.e. eventually propel the frisbee through the goal or at the tree. The winner is the thrower with the lowest score. The pace of the game tends to be fast as the thrower will usually run after the frisbee to make the second or third throw before the interceptors have positioned themselves. One other rule: the thrower must launch the frisbee from where it has landed from the previous throw and 'catchers' may not move the frisbee except after a catch or in an attempt to make a catch. They may 'stop' a rolling frisbee.

THREE AND IN

Taking the principle of most 3 or 4 player football games, the frisbee can be used as the ball while one player acts as goalkeeper. Goalposts are ideal, but two sturdy trees can be used with equal success. The players each have one throw in turn and the first player to beat the goalie three times gets a turn in goal. A handicapping system based on age and ability can easily be introduced by setting different shortest distances from which each player can shoot.

SWING BALL
(Manufacturer: Dunlop)

Swing ball is a competitive 2 player racket game, which can be used indoors or out. It is available from most sports shops and consists of a base (which is filled with sand or water for stability) and a pole which fits into the base. The top of the pole is fitted with a spiral device which enables a tennis ball on a string to be attached. When the string is positioned in the centre of the spiral, the ball can then be hit (2 rackets are supplied) around the pole several times in either direction without the string fouling.

Swing Ball is played with the competitors facing each other with the pole between them. The string is maneouvred to the centre of the spiral and one person is nominated to commence play by hitting the ball in a clockwise direction around the pole. The second player hits anti-clockwise, trying to reverse the direction of play and so force the string down the spiral, until it fouls, thus defeating their opponent. Swing Ball is an energetic game, which can be played quite skillfully by most adolescents. It is an ideal family game.

OUTDOOR BOULES

Vaguely similar to British green bowls, this outdoor version is of French derivation. Sets of 6 balls and 2 jacks are obtained from good sports shops. Metal sets are expensive - plastic is cheaper and quite adequate for most purposes.

Usually restricted to 2 or 3 players, the jack is positioned 1-20 feet away from the base. Players take it in turn to lob (not roll) their 2 or 3 boules at the jack. The person whose boule is nearest to the jack scores one 'shot' plus an extra one for each of their boules that is closer to the jack than the nearest of their opponents'. The second jack can be positioned at base, and play resumes for the next round. A useful piece of equipment to have handy when spending time outdoors, e.g. at a campsite, barbecue or family gathering.

INDOOR BOWLS

Such equipment is expensive to buy, but can usually be found in community centres. Simply an indoor version of green bowls, a pile carpet is necessary to play on. Bowls is a fascinating game and it's worth trying it at least once in a group's life, to see if it catches on. Remember, though, that it's a very poor substitute for green bowling which can be tried for real during the summer months.

CAN REACH

This falls into the 'short diversion' category of games. It involves the use of matched drinks cans as platforms for the hands. Members of either sex can be involved and it's basically like doing press-ups on short hand stilts. Using a line on the floor, (a carpeted surface works best) contestants have their toes behind the line and have to move their hands forward to the furthest extent possible, whilst clutching a can in each. Altogether, a painful bit of sado-masochism, yet daft enough to appeal to the humour of young and old. For variety, you might suggest participants trying to do a few press-ups from the extended position; for competitive purposes, the winner is the person who can stretch the furthest, toes behind the line and hands perched on cans. You might even suggest that each person trying has to hand-walk their cans back to the base-line!

VELCRO CATCH BALL
(Various manufacturers)
Rather like a plague of extra-terrestrial beasties, luridly-coloured velcro gloves and hand held catching discs have caused a veritable infestation in the UK's parks, beaches and playing fields. The games themselves are an elaborated form of catch. Two or more players throw the ball between them, catching the ball on the velcro pads. It's more fun than watching paint dry, and although the velcro quite quickly loses its adhesion value, the playing sets are usually cheap to buy. As young people used to enjoy playing 'Sling Ball', the Velcro version is a natural successor and a good game for mixed age groups, families and all kinds of youth groups.

To vary the game, various ways of scoring can be used, including the old-fashioned system of penalties such as getting down on one knee and then two knees for a subsequent missed catch.

HUMAN CHAIR

Also known as the 'Lap Sit' in New Games, this is a fun sequence for medium to large sized groups. Age is immaterial, but players must be fit enough to handle taking a possible tumble.

The games organiser invites all the participants to stand in a line. Next, starting at the front of the line, each person in the line sits down on the knees of the person behind them, turning the whole line into one, long, human chair. With a little practice and the odd collapse, the human chair can be taught to walk, and to lift up all its left legs or right legs. Good fun to watch, and even better fun to participate in, the Human Chair is a very popular non-competitive activity.

MUSICAL CHAIRS

This was brought to our attention through Mike from Tayside who is one of the keenest exponents of 'New Games' in Scotland. It's ideal for an end of the session, closing exercise. Played using the new rules, it leaves everyone grinning, exhausted and feeling suitably 'child-like'. It can be used with any age group and is highly recommended for mixed age groups and on a large scale. About 15 is probably the minimum number, for the impact of the sequence to be felt. As in ordinary 'Musical Chairs', you set out one chair each, minus one, for the participants in the first round, but it is best if you organise the chairs of the stacking, or school room variety, in a snake, alternately facing opposite ways. The cavorting dancers can then skip round the entire snake of chairs until the music stops. The first round begins to demonstrate the difference. You, as leader, tell the person who looks like being left out, "find a lap!" to ensure that no-one is 'out'. But you keep on reducing the chairs in each round, ending up with massive, snaking lap sits attached to only a very small number of chairs. We saw the sequence with about 70 players balanced on laps, sort of attached to four or five chairs. A nice way to end on a 'high' note!

Notes.

Section Seven:
COMMERCIAL
GAMES

INTRODUCTION

Commercial games come in all shapes and sizes. Some are boxed and expensively packaged; others are little more than a bat and a ball (or two!). And, at the most expensive end of things are the computer games consoles, virtual reality and hand-held games, which now rival arcade machines for sophistication of speed and graphics. Why should we bother ourselves about them in the **New Youth Games Book** ? Our strong conviction is that almost all games can be used to develop relationships, and provide a platform for adults and young people and groups of young people themselves to have some fun, and possibly do a bit of learning along the way!

We originally included a section on commercial games in the earlier Youth Games Book. We have tried to update and amend this to reflect changes in play in the 1990's. But, we have still retained some 'old faithfuls' like Boggle, Scrabble and Monopoly. We are not expert enough to really comment in-depth on the arcade-type games, especially since the scene is rapidly developing with new technology, and games appearing weekly or at least monthly. Suffice it to say that many children and young people are hooked on these type of games and rather than rejecting them as being mindless, it is better to try and use them as group activities, promoting interaction and shared fun.

For those of you who run youth clubs and similar, we would repeat our earlier plea that games should not be regarded as something to be kept hidden in the back of the store cupboard. Boxed games of the commercial variety tend to be scorned and neglected. Few see the light of day and rarely have we seen youth and/or group workers involving themselves in playing such games. The consequence is that commercial games are rarely utilised as a resource. Rules are not learned, pieces are lost, and too often the playing pieces become missiles to be chucked around on a boring club night. The same can happen in schools and in the home.

The obvious answer is for adults to make an effort to keep an eye open for new games, spend some time learning the rules and **then** to share this knowledge with the young people around them. Another idea which is worth considering is to contact some of your local toy shops. Many shops will offer good discounts to youth groups, and if their staff are knowledgeable, they will probably be able to advise on games which might be suitable for particular age groups and applications. Within our own jobs, we tried to 'test' out different games in the variety of settings where we worked. Whether it was in a youth centre or a social work group, no-one was ever compelled to play, but we did actively try and encourage participation in a spirit of enthusiasm and exploration. We tried to be a part of the games and by actively participating, the more positive use of games developed in an unhurried, spontaneous sort of way. We used them to involve youngsters with each other, and it offered a way in which we could give individual youngsters a bit of extra attention. Even single player games like the maze puzzles can become group activities: "Can **you** do it, Howie?" or "How do you play this or Alan?"

Unlike in the other sections of the book, **we have not tried to offer sets of rules and tips on play**. In no sense do we intend to infringe copyright, nor do we think that rules without the playing pieces or board are particularly useful. Instead we have tried to offer:

- comments on the appropriateness of different games in different settings.
- our responses and comments on which games seem suitable for adults to use with young people to help develop relationships and acquire some literacy and numeracy skills, or expand dexterity.
- suggestions of games which we have found easy for young people to learn and are fun in the playing.

Some games which we have **not included,** we found too long for use in youth group settings or schools. We've enjoyed playing fantasy role-playing games of the Dungeons and Dragons variety, and lengthy board games such as Risk and Diplomacy, but they are too complicated and time consuming for most youth work situations.

One useful tip to have in mind, is that many of the games we have written about can be passed on, using monitor style procedures, with one youngster explaining how to play to their friends and other games players. You should also try out some of your own favourite games. We have not included chess, backgammon or Go, for instance. If an adult is enthusiastic about a particular game, this enthusiasm can often be successfully passed on to young people, resulting in them being 'hooked' on that game.

We hope that this chapter completes the total picture of games playing with young people. Our only major omission is the organised, traditional team game and sports. Many of these must not be discounted since they provide plenty of opportunities for young and old to share a love of sport, and to get rid of excess energy and aggression. For instance, Alan does a lot of cross-country running, where the spirit of competition, comradeship and participation is very strong; much as in a good games session.

UNO
(Manufacturer: Mattel)
This is a card game which has virtually conquered the games playing world. Where Alan lives these days in Dorset, there is a thriving Uno club, where ten year olds play alongside their much older colleagues. The game is fast, noisy and seems to create a good atmosphere. In Britain, the game is now marketed by Mattel, following on, we believe, from Waddingtons. We first met up with

the game while holidaying in Spain and Italy and think that the game originates from one of these countries. There is also a Uno Rummy game.

TELL ME
(Manufacturer: Spears)
This is a quiz game which has certainly been around for all of our forty-something lives! The box contains a spinner which displays letters of the alphabet and a set of question cards, with two levels of question. The idea is for one person to control the spinner and the quiz cards, reading out the letter and question along the lines:
"Tell me a type of bird beginning with C."
In the rules, it suggests that the first person to answer the question wins the card. We have also played 'Tell Me' by taking turns, which makes it easier for the simpler or harder questions to be used for participants of different ages and abilities. In older sets, there was only one level of question. Make sure you buy a set with the two levels of question. Recommended both as a simple learning aid and for good, old-fashioned fun!

PICTIONARY
(Manufacturer: Parker)
This combines drawing and wordplay. The aim of the game is to have participants sketch a drawing which represents words and phrases. It is not that easy, but can offer plenty of amusement for a group with reasonable literacy levels. Basically, it's an artistic derivation of charades.

BLOCKBUSTERS & CHAIN LETTERS
(Manufacturers: Waddingtons and Spears, respectively)
These are two of the better TV game spin-offs into the commercial, boxed games market. You're probably more familiar with the TV versions than we are! Both are word games, and as such need to be treated with caution depending upon the literacy levels of the young people playing them. We rather preferred Blockbusters, but would suggest that both are worth investigating if you want a different word game. Both are most suitable for the twelve plus age range.

CLOSE THE BOX
(Various manufacturers)
This is a traditional game, re-packaged for commercial sale. As a teaching aid it is a good introduction to numbers and at the same time seems to be popular with most young people. A simple idea, the box has the numbers 1 to 9 inscribed along the inside and above each number is a flap which can be turned over to cover the number. Two dice are thrown and the total indicates the value of flaps which can be closed up. Say, a total of 9 is thrown, then any of the following combinations of flaps may be closed.

$$9 = 8+1; 7+2; 6+3; 2+7; 5+4; 5+3+1; \text{ and } 4+3+2.$$

That player continues to throw the 2 dice until either they cannot use part of the total score, or all the flaps have been turned over. In the version we used, 6 small ball-bearings are provided for each player. The numbers left uncovered at the end of the game give the numbers of balls to be given to the opponent. At the end of a turn, the other player repeats the process.

It sounds mundane, and it is, but it has a strange sort of appeal, and can be played by any age and takes just as long as the contestants want it to. There are quite cheap versions of the game on the market, and if you go for a strong one it should last for years. Sometimes, sets are given away as promotional prizes.

SUBBUTEO FOOTBALL
(Manufacturer: Subbuteo Football)
Our friend, Alberto, persuaded us to include this one as a good game for the more organised youth club. Played on a five foot long green cloth the game involves 'finger-tip' control of the 11-a-side football teams which compete for a fixed period of time; 2 halves, say, perhaps ten minutes each way. Set out on a table top, with the cloth firmly held down, the game can be played by a number of participants and features all the normal rules of football, goals, penalties, fouls, throw-ins etc.

Club-championships have been organised in some youth centres, and a league-table structure could be established where the game is popular. Probably the better mannered members of some youth organisations are the most likely players for this game or its near relation, the table top war games. These again require special equipment, soldiers, dice and rulers - but you'll have to read about the finer points elsewhere!

Returning to Subbuteo football, our advice is to consider buying the 'Club Edition', which has all the basics without the extra paraphernalia gone in for by the enthusiast.

LEGOLAND/TECHNICS
(Manufacturer: Lego)
The wonderful world of Legoland takes some beating in terms of educational and play value for children and young people. The magic, enjoyment and fun value of lego never really fades, and it can act as a useful passport back to the half-forgotten childhood for many adolescents. This is especially useful in situations such as bereavement and counselling work.

For youth groups, buying individual packs of lego can be rather expensive. However, many families and some schools have built up plentiful stocks of lego, and 'jumbles' and 'appeals' can often raise the necessary starter stock of pirates, galleons, houses, castles, space police, racing cars and harbours. Lego, and the more complex 'Technic' vehicles sets, are all useful for impromptu individual and group construction sessions. It can provide the means for a quiet individual break, or the focus for fevered group activity. Quite a play resource, with lots of potential for learning along the way.

REBOUND
(Manufacturer: Ideal)
An activity game; this is closely allied to the traditional game of Shuffleboard. Produced in quite sturdy plastic with metal, low-friction playing pieces, the game is at least strong enough to be 'let out' unsupervised. In the following diagram the shape of the board and the path of movement for the players' 4 pieces are shown.

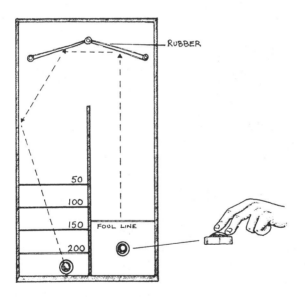

Pieces are pushed up the table and the two-players shove one piece alternately up the board. The rubbers at the top end of the board act as a cushion and the pieces re-bound down the left-hand passage into the scoring area. Only pieces inside each scoring line area count, so, part of the game is to nudge your own pieces on to score and push the opponent out.

It seems to be appreciated as an activity wherever we tried it. Like other games we've used, it produced its own waiting list and queue of users. The sides of the board are used as a score board and it can be played either by 2 players, or in teams. We got bored by it rather quickly, but the same was not apparent amongst the younger users. It's funny but if the same board had been made of a nice block of teak, I think that we adults would like the game more. People are strange! But, perhaps that could be the incentive to make a 'nicer' version.

MASTERMIND
(Manufacturer: Invicta)
Suffice it to say that most people have played this 2 player game at some time. The basic principle involves hiding 4 coloured pegs under a shield and then the other player tries to find out the hidden sequence by testing coloured pegs and being told non-verbally by the placing of black and white pegs, whether any are in the correct sequence. After about 8 tries, normally a player finds the original combination.

Nowadays, most of the youngsters have seen and played Mastermind a bit too often and although the original idea is a unique one, it has paled somewhat with over-use. Suggestions for **variations** which we have tried are (1) to add 3 or 4 extra colours, or (2) combining 2 boards together to play a double game with a code combination of 8. Both make for a more difficult game, but not doubly difficult; it usually takes about 30% more tries to find tries to find the winning line. (3) consecutive games can be played with two boards.

Age-wise, we would reckon 9 or 10 upwards; the time for a game of one guess each is about 15 minutes.

There are also word and number versions of the basic game but we feel that the rather poor quality pieces might easily get lost with youngsters using them.

BOGGLE
(Manufacturer: Palitoy)
Boggle has become, quite rapidly, one of the biggest selling word games on the market. What is more crucial, it has proved itself to be a popular game in youth groups. Even while buying our new set of 'Boggle' from John Menzies in Glasgow, a local youth leader came in for an extra set, extolling the virtues of the game. Being a word game, like Scrabble, youngsters are automatically learning as they play the quick-fire sequence of three and more letter, 'word making.' Letters are printed on each face of sixteen cubes. These are then shaken up in a covered container. The lid is taken off and each participant races against a sand-timer to write down as many words which they can spot amongst the 4 x 4 square of letter cubes. The 'hidden' words can be made out of the letters reading forwards, backwards, diagonally and even round corners, making the game almost an exercise in lateral thinking. Highly recommended!

BAGATELLE
(Various manufacturers)
This was a Victorian pastime and the wooden tables, normally made with a semi-circular top are available either through the games and toy shops or in secondhand shops, where £5 may get you an antique as well as an enjoyable game. The idea, which has been translated into simpler, plastic copies, is to knock (or in some versions, shoot with a spring-trigger) ball bearings into a variety of cup-holes and segmented areas made from tacks nailed into the board. Most boards look something like:

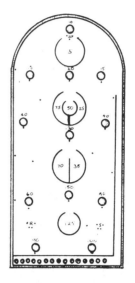

The balls are knocked around the board and when all have been used the score is totalled and other contestants have their turns. About 3 turns each with up to 4 players makes for a good game. It is refreshing to see youngsters getting pleasure from an old-fashioned pastime. We were lucky in having 2 other early twentieth century bagatelle type games. They were more like prototypes for pin-ball and therefore, if anything, were even more popular.

Kids of all ages enjoyed the game and although it might not be a piece of equipment you would want to use every week, the acquisition of bagatelle can be a boon. New models tend to cost £20 plus and are made of a far inferior wood to old models, so the junk shop suggestion can be beneficial.

WATER GAMES
(Manufacturer: Tomy)
We are not going to suggest drowning all the kids in your care although you may sometimes (often?) feel so inclined! Instead, the water games we are referring to are various shaped boxes filled with water. There are now dozens of varieties on the market. We found all intrigued, some were much more skilful.

Pushing the button on the front of the box sends a stream of water into the container which moves balls, rings or whatever around. The aim then is to manoeuvre these missiles into or onto targets. It's more difficult than it sounds and quite addictive if not used in isolation from alternative pastimes.

Youngsters can compete using the games singly and then comparing the scores. Most of the games have an 'out of play' area, so scoring can be counted **against** each player. Not a bad investment, since they seem to be fairly well made, and as long as they are not used as the ball in netball or touch rugby, they should survive a school year, or so.

SCRABBLE
(Manufacturer: Spears)
This old game has become one of the most beloved of family recreations. We have also found that most projects and centres we visit have sets and use them. The game, as most people know, involves placing words, one letter to each tile onto a board with marked squares. These squares on the board indicate when the score of words are doubled or trebled and likewise with individual letter tiles, which are each numbered. Words must join on to letters of words already on the board. The winner is the person who has the highest score when the tiles run out at the end of the game.

Most children from about 7 upwards, can, in a limited way play Scrabble, but in adult company (up to 4 can play) they'll get a mite hammered. So, with kids holding a limited vocabulary we use a 4 or 5 **maximum letters** in a word rule, or use the Junior Scrabble version. However, Junior Scrabble is pretty tedious for adults, so we prefer to use the full version. This extra rule acts as a leveller, although it obviously decreases the enjoyment for the adults. A good painless way to increase the vocabulary. We found that the game worked better in the slightly quieter environment of group work rather than in a youth club setting. The game does last a bit longer than we would normally recommend for kids' groups, probably in the order of one and a half hours, but only an hour where kids play without adults. These older people even 'ruin' Scrabble, you see!

If a club is **into** games at any level, Scrabble is a must. Interestingly, Spears have also built a market with Scrabble spin-offs. As well as Junior Scrabble, there are Scrabble Dice and Scrabble Rebus and Travel Scrabble. Scrabble Dice is a fast version of the basic game, but we found the rules a bit boring, since the player who throws the dice can be too obvious in their choice of word, which means that everyone copies it! Like in Boggle, play is governed by using an egg timer.

MONOPOLY and CLUEDO
(Manufacturer: Waddington)
In many ways, these are the 'dodos' of the Games Scene. Both are still purchased consistently and provide hours of fun and aggravation. In the case of Monopoly it literally is hours and hours, and we always use either the shortened version mentioned in the Waddington rules, where 2 properties are dealt immediately to each player and a time limit is established, or a version where 4 properties are given to each player which **they don't have to pay for**. This moves the game on by about three quarters of an hour. Monopoly, because it is universally known, can still provide a valuable group experience. The interaction which takes place may lead to the same sort of debriefing and group discussion which we have talked about in the relationship games section.

Cluedo is a short game, played in twenty minute sequences and involves deducing who is the criminal, what implement they used for the crime, and where it took place. The movement around the board is made by dice throw and then one hears improbable statements such as: "I suspect Colonel Mustard in the study with a rope". This is inevitably followed by a humorist who will say: "I suspect the Reverend Green with Miss Scarlet with a candlestick." It's a good game and although the rules take a few minutes to explain, it's not difficult to learn.

STAY ALIVE
(Manufacturer: M. & B. Games)
This is one of those infuriating games where you and the youngsters you are playing with will always be 'almost winning'. It's not a very serious game, therefore it almost falls into the category of 'non-competitive,' since whatever strenuous efforts you make to cause the opponents' balls to disappear, you seem equally likely to commit hara-kiri and join the ranks of seasoned 'Exit' members! The nature of the game is simple; between 2 and 4 players distribute their sets of marbles across the board which is riddled with holes. The exact position of the holes is controlled by each player sliding the horizontal and vertical plastic slides one notch along in an attempt to aid the disappearance of enemy marbles. The result is a quick game which is nicely unpredictable. It's a well made product, and in our experience stood up well to youth group rigours and only the marbles needed replacing. We are on our third set!

MAZES

(Various makes)

The traditional ball bearing puzzle was a popular toy in the period between the First and Second World Wars. Mazes were made to represent all sorts of scenarios, including the advance of the British troops in world war I, a round of golf and motor races. In the sixties and seventies the ideas were revived, using clear plastic casings. Many of these involved balancing the small ball-bearing on a raised ledge and manipulating it around the raised path to the end. Others used the old fashioned pathway principle where the aim is to avoid falling down the holes cut into the pathway. Pocketeers have recently introduced one such model where a path is followed and the ball must be moved into a small

boat and across a river, up and over bridges and through other hazards. It's not the best made puzzle we have seen, but it's a good idea and we would recommend the **Pocketeers** as a range of small, cheap toys worth considering. The only drawback we can see is that being small, they also fit neatly into small pockets, leaving buildings!

The time taken to complete a puzzle or do and re-do it is unlimited, depending on the patience and determination of the user. The Los Imposibles puzzle by Congost of Spain is one we have seen 19 year old bikers spend an evening fiddling with, and a five year old girl complete in five minutes! They are very personal things and can be thought of as annoying and frustrating by some youngsters and adults.

At the top end of the range are the Swedish wood mazes, Tomy's beat the clock and King Kong mazes, and 'Round the Bend' made in plastic by Invicta. All are relatively expensive.

We liked the way that the mazes could be used. They can be left on tables and passed around between youngsters, and they don't require the setting up or rule learning of other games. Also they can be played between any number, age or ability range of youngsters (and adults). The: "Want to see if you can beat me at this?" invitation from a staff member will often work where other ways of starting a conversation have failed.

YAHTZEE
(Manufacturer: M. & B. **Games)**
Ingenious, simple and hybrid. Sounding more like a description in a rose catalogue, rather than a game, Yahtzee has its roots (excuse the pun) in Poker dice and simple scoring games. Although it is a so-called 'Commercial Game,' the only equipment needed is a set of 5 standard dice and a pad of score sheets, one of which is given to each player. Unlike some other games in this section, it can be played by any number from 2 to 6 with equal success.

We found that it worked in a variety of group settings, both formal and informal. A game lasts about half an hour and once learned it is an easy game to just 'leave about,' and then, with the minimum of supervision the monitor principle takes over, one youngster explaining the rules to the others.

As in Bridge, (for games freaks), the scoring is achieved in 2 sections above and below the line. Each player throws the 5 dice and tries to 'score' in a section of the scoring table which hasn't been filled in. Any number of dice can be thrown 3 times and then either a section must be scored or a section is 'blocked in', indicating that the player cannot or does not want to make a score elsewhere on the pad. The sections to be scored are Aces; Twos; Threes; etc and then as in Poker dice, straight runs; full house; 3 & 4 of a kind and Yahtzee, which is 5 of a particular number, say 5 x 3s. A score over 63 in the '1-6 section', above the line, gives a Bonus score of 35. Every section must, by the end of the game, be 'scored' or 'blocked off'. The winner, predictably, is the person with the highest score. There are other rules, but that's the basics. A good game which is quite skilful, but once watched it is usually easy enough for kids to master.

TWISTER

(Manufacturer: M. & B. Games)
With action all the way, Twister is most definitely a 'doing game'. Played in stockinged feet, the contestants entangle themselves and one another on a plastic sheet playing surface marked up with coloured circles.

A master of ceremonies calls out a colour and part of the anatomy, left or right hand, or foot, to be placed on a paticular colour. The decision is made mechanically by a spin of an arrow. The end result of the proceedings is a knotted, laughing heap of bodies. The number of players in sessions which we were organising varied between 2 and 6. When we weren't involved, the apparatus tended to be used as the means to get into the Guinness Book of Records, with upwards of ten folk piled, pyramid-style towards the ceiling!

Great as a 'one-off', we also found some indication that the game could be played on a regular basis for 3 or 4 sessions. In itself a fun idea, the commercial game, like its close-relation, 'Get Knotted', can be used to break down some of the physical inhibitions of group members.

COMPUTER GAMES MACHINES

Back in the Computer Dark Ages we both spent endless hours using and developing games and training aids for the BBC micro.

Nowadays, we play the occasional round of golf or game of chess on the 486 PC, but have not kept fully abreast of changes in the computer games console marketplace. So, apologies out of the way, we will try our best to offer a few ideas and hints.

As we have already mentioned, the main problem is the speed of developments in this field. What was 'state of the art' six months ago is now a dodo. There seem to be three main types of games machine. The first is the most familiar to us; it's the personal computer complete with a keyboard, joystick and any necessary add-ons, such as paddles, gun and sound links. The second, and probably the fastest growing sector is the games console which come in a vast array of non-compatible formats. The third format is the hand held games machine.

USING GAMES ON COMPUTERS

The Amiga and Atari ST range of computers have led the way in this sector of the games market, partly, we'd guess, because parents with the purchasing power believed they were buying a 'proper' computer. Both boast a good range of games. Many young people have inherited older computers which run games as well as business software. These range from the various BBC machines through to the Spectrum and Commodore. By current standards, the operating speed, quality of graphics and complexity of these machines is primitive, but if the games themselves were well constructed they can still provide a lot of fun, and as with all games have a social and educational side as well.

All IBM compatible computers will run games software which can be bought either on floppy disc, or, increasingly on CD discs. Shareware, which is fundamentally cheaper and older versions of games and other software can be purchased quite reasonably, especially on CD, where 12,000 programs may only cost £50 - the catch being you then have to work through the menus and programs to see what you've got!

GAMES CONSOLES

Up until now games consoles have been relatively cheap at about £100-£150, but each game can then cost up to £60! Sega, Nintendo and Atari are the best known names in this field, with the likes of Panasonic now entering the arena. Since none of them are compatible, and with new games requiring 50 meg and more of memory space, the new generation of machines coming over from America are expensive. Atari are backing the cartridge based Jaguar and Panasonic, the REAL 3DO, which doubles as a CD player. Both claim to bring 'reality' (virtual or otherwise!) into the home.

A hard-sell through the computer magazines and on the box will probably make most of the nation's young computer games-freaks feel that their Mega Drives and Master Systems and Atari ST are a mite old fashioned. Parents and youth workers probably need to seek advice from young experts regarding both current systems and software.

HAND-HELD SYSTEMS

Game Boy, Lynx and Game Gear are three of the most popular systems. Various devices are available to make them compatible with their larger cousins in the games module market. When trying some of the games we found the small screens and the cramped graphics irritating, and the small buttons favour younger fingers than our own! For any sort of group interaction, we feel that the hand-held machines are not an option.

SOFTWARE

The word 'software' covers all of the games cartridges, floppy discs, and CD's on which a game may be introduced to the computer or games playing machine. We have used a lot of different games and have our own preferences. Increasingly, games are interactive, allowing the player(s) to make changes to the structure of the game and to alter the way in which the game works. CD-i (pronounced CD-eye!) is one of the latest developments and in its most sophisticated form allows the user to write new programs onto a CD disc. Some of the latest games integrate video sequences where the players can role-play the characters in the plot and change the outcomes in the film by making choices. It's a far cry from playing space-invaders or table tennis on the home TV screen!

We have looked particularly for games which are not purely the shoot 'em-jump over them - crunch them type of arcade action. We also like games where there is a mixture of manual keyboard or joystick dexterity, coupled with decision-making which stretches the brain cells a bit! Broadly, games fall into a range of categories:

1. **Arcade games**. These require fast reactions and often involve fighting against cartoon characters; outshooting and outkicking ; finding a way through a fantasy world. A second type simulate motor racing, aerial combat, tank battles or similar. The most sophisticated and probably interesting, combine fast reactions with strategic decision making. A number of flight/navigation simulators also integrate some interesting aspects of multiple choice, and at the time of writing, Electronic Arts: Wing Commander, Privateer is a popular front runner. More mind-warping than, say, Sonic 3!

2. **Adventure Games**. These are a development of fantasy game playing, but with the added advantage of good graphics. They usually pit the player(s) against a range of enemies who try and prevent the participants reaching their quest, which can be anything from solving a murder to slaying the dragon.

3. **Strategic games**. Many of these are based on well known board games or war-gaming. Chess, draughts, backgammon and even Jack the Ripper have made the transition to the computer game screen.

4. Decision-making games. These describe real life situations such as running a football team, or even a youth club. The game is then structured offering a number of choices and options which are meant to simulate the real life outcomes.

5. Quizzes and Board Games. Many of the most popular board games have made the transition to the computer. Trivial Pursuits and Monopoly are two of the well-known and loved examples.

6. Sports simulations. There are sports simulations of just about every sport. Golf and motor racing are two of the most popular, but I'm sure that if you want a simulation of hot-air ballooning that there is one somewhere!

As with other commercial games, try and get advice (preferably not from the computer salesperson) on what to look at, or consider buying. Some suppliers will let bona fide youth groups try out software on approval, and some offer a rental system.

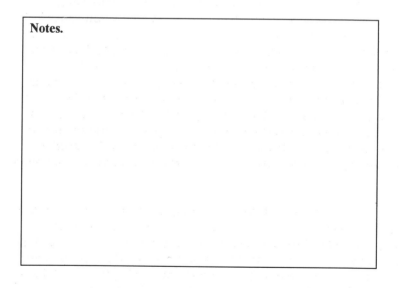

Notes.

Section Eight:
SIMULATIONS

"In the beginning .... " as all good books say, we mentioned that we are not one hundred and one per cent 'sold' on the use of simulations and role plays at every opportunity. Some of our professional colleagues like Tom Scott, who helped towards this collection are convinced and use the techniques at many staff development sessions and interestingly in I.T. group work and in training and fun sessions with youngsters in the 14-20 age group. They could also be used in a classroom, or even at home with a group of youngsters wanting a 'challenge'.

Anyway, our sour grapes out of the way, we would like to commend 'Star Power' and the 'Tower Game' to you as well-honed training simulations ideal for conferences, team meetings and the like. Both require briefing and de-briefing and a certain quantity of equipment as listed in the game descriptions. Starpower is analogous to the class struggle or just keeping one's head above the water-line. It is designed to arouse strong emotions, so don't think that it is your handling of the group if participants opt out and temporarily disappear. Acquisition and doing down your neighbour and some measure of knowledge concerning how rules are made and broken all come into a normal session.

In contrast, the Tower Game is a group exercise with the groups locked into competition with one another to build the most financially advantageous tower. The game is well worth playing with older kids' groups as well as in a staff context. As a 'doing' exercise, it is fun, and a good, money producing tower will have involved the builders in an amount of lateral thinking.

'News at Ten' requires at least one video recording/playback outfit and, as you might expect, simulates the 'behind the scenes' action in a television news broadcasting studio. With a group, committed to 'give it a try', it can very accurately reflect the stress and 'organised chaos' of television news production. 'News at Ten' generates a wealth of discussion on the factors necessary for good team work.

STAR POWER
And after Star Trek and Star Wars, here it is, Star Power!

You will need the following equipment:
(1) Supplies of coloured tiddlywinks (or counters of some sort).
(2) Copies of the rules of bargaining.
(3) Blackboard and chalk or flip chart and markers.
(4) Badge labels showing triangles, circles and squares.

See Rules of Bargaining for values of the counters (tiddlywinks etc.).

INTRODUCTION
This is a very powerful simulation which can generate strong feelings for participants. These feelings are the crux of the simulation and must be thoroughly discussed during the subsequent debriefing. The role of the organiser is crucial: you must be fully conversant with the method of play and the rules of bargaining; you must also use a directive style of leadership and be prepared to confront the many challenges you'll receive during play.

Star Power is essentially a trading game where players trade counters to maximise their score (the objective set for each participant). However, each player's chance of scoring well is largely determined by the value of the counters they are originally given .... and this is carefully arranged to create three groups, or 'classes'. 'Squares' have tokens of high value; 'Circles' of medium value, and 'Triangles' of low value.

METHOD OF PLAY
Divide the group into three, labelling members of each sub-group

as squares, triangles or circles. Distribute 5 counters to each person. Load the total value of counters to favour squares, with less to circles and much less to triangles. It's a good idea to prepare counters beforehand, putting each person's in a small plastic bag or twist of paper.

Carefully explain the Rules of Bargaining, and answer any questions from participants before opening the first trading session. During trading make sure that the Rules of Bargaining are adhered to .... exclude transgressors from one or more trading sessions, depending on how nasty you feel !

RULES OF BARGAINING

After each trading session, send participants back into their groups and put individual scores on the blackboard under these groupings. Without stating any reason, give each group three counters telling them that each scores twenty points, and the counters may be divided between three people, two people, or all given to one person. When these new scores are put on the board (members who have received some or all of the sixty points have their scores changed) re-arrange the groups so that those with the highest scores go into squares, any low ones go into triangles, and the rest go into circles. Try to keep the groups reasonably even in size. (When members change groups they must, of course, change their labels as well.) Take back the counters worth twenty points and repeat the process of 'trading sessions' and scoring as long as you like.

Participants tend to go through **three stages:**
(a) This is a joke but I will go along with it.
(b) I'm a bit involved but it's only a game.
(c) I really mind about what is happening.

After about 3 or 4 rounds, when the squares have thoroughly established themselves, you can allow them to make one or more new rules (e.g. they may change the value of the currency, or they may make new trading rules). You may then, if you wish, after another round or two, turn the tables on the powerful squares, by allowing the triangles to make a rule change. The tendency is usually for the squares to make a rule change which reinforces their economic power, while the triangles tend to go for a more egalitarian approach.

You must decide how long to allow the game to continue. This will depend on how much feeling you want to generate, and you **must** allow time for debriefing and reflection.

RULES OF BARGAINING

1. You have TEN MINUTES to improve your scores.
2. You improve scores by trading advantageously with others.
3. Persons must be holding hands to effect a trade.
4. Only one-for-one trades are legal. Two for one or any other combinations are illegal.
5. Once you touch the hand of another participant, a counter of **unequal** value or colour must be traded. If a couple cannot consummate a trade they have to hold hands for the rest of the ten minute trading session .
6. NO TALKING MAY TAKE PLACE UNLESS HANDS ARE TOUCHING.
7. Persons with folded arms do NOT have to trade with other persons.
8. ALL COUNTERS MUST BE HIDDEN.
9. Value of counters:

> BLUE   50 POINTS
> PINK   25 POINTS
> GREEN 15 POINTS
> YELLOW 10 POINTS
> WHITE   5 POINTS

5 counters of same colour - extra 25
4 counters of same colour - extra 15
3 counters of same colour - extra 10
2 counters of same colour - 0

Points to consider during debriefing

What are the:
(1) Comparisons with real social structures?
(2) Assumptions of going up and down? (i.e. improving your score means getting **more** points, the squares **win** etc).
(3) Feelings of participants about moving from group to group, or not being able to move, or not wanting to move, opting out etc.?
(4) Reasons behind who keeps to the rules and who doesn't?
(5) What rules do the squares or triangles change and why?

THE TOWER GAME
Budding Basil Spence enthusiasts are especially welcome in this game!

You may consider offering a pre-arranged incentive (small prize) which can be awarded to the winning group. To operate the simulation with four groups, you require a minimum of 200 eight-blob lego bricks and four base plates, plus the following rules, graphs and incentive charts.

The **aim of the game** is for each group to work as a team and produce the **highest tower in the fastest time using the fewest bricks.** Extra **PROFIT** will be gained by teams who estimate accurately the height, bricks and time they will need to build their Tower.

There are **two phases** in the game:

Phase 1: Groups are chosen and in a period of up to an hour the groups work separately on the tasks indicated in the Planning Phase.
Phase 2: This is the Construction Phase and the time allowed for the simulation is the number of groups multiplied by 20 minutes.

1. PLANNING

The groups may join bricks together, but these must be pulled apart before entering the Construction Phase. Each group is given a collection of LEGO including base plate and approximately 50 bricks. The group tasks are to:

(a) Run tests on possible tower designs.
(b) Draw a design of the tower to be built indicating the method of joining the bricks.
(c) Estimate the profit (see separate estimate chart and incentive graphs), time taken, height of tower and bricks used.
(d) Make a plan/description of who is expected to take what part in the Construction Phase.

2. CONSTRUCTION
Up to 20 minutes will be allowed for each group to carry out the following tasks:
1) Introduce and describe the plan.
2) Brief group members.
3) Build the tower (stop-watch timed) using the base plate and 200 bricks.

4) Measure the completed work against the estimates and the incentive graphs to arrive at a **profit record**.

After all teams have engaged in the construction activity, the team with the highest profit record is declared the winner and group discussion, as desired, can take place.

The profit record is the total profit gained in incentives for speed, height, careful use of materials and bonuses for accurate estimates.

INCENTIVE GRAPHS

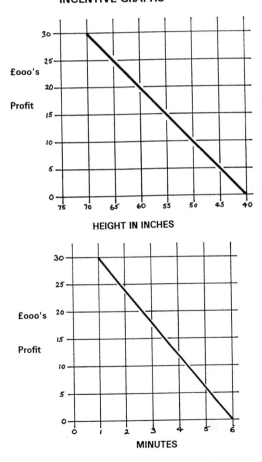

HEIGHT IN INCHES

MINUTES

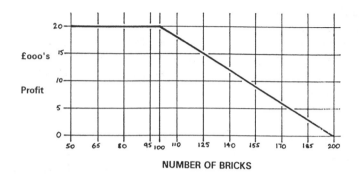

NUMBER OF BRICKS

ESTIMATES

Estimates regarding height, time and bricks used carry the following *bonus profits:*

Height	40-59"	51-60"	61-75"
Accurate within 7"	£3,000	£4,000	£5,000
Accurate within 3"	£4,000	£5,000	£6,000
Time	Under 1 min	1-3 mins	4-6 mins
Accurate within 10 secs	£6,000	£4,000	£3,000
Accurate within 30 secs	£4,000	£3,000	£2,000
Bricks	151-200	101-150	Under 100
Accurate within 10 bricks	£2,000	£3,000	£5,000
Accurate within 5 bricks	£3,000	£5,000	£6,000

NEWS AT TEN

This simulation is always chaotic (mirroring the drama and stress of television news production) but is guaranteed to be great fun! The task, for a group of 8 or more, is to prepare and present a 10 minute news broadcast. Not as easy as it sounds, especially as the 10 minute 'News at Ten' broadcast is recorded on video tape for a hilarious playback experience.

Although it is suitable for use with a well-established group of young people, the simulation is also an excellent staff training tool. It can be used to stimulate debate and greater clarity about issues such as collaborative working, role differentiation, task management and leadership.

WHAT YOU NEED

A selection of clippings from newspapers and magazines. Include news items from both local and national newspapers as this reflects the range of material used in news broadcasting. Make sure you have a few 'serious' news items of national importance as well as some 'general interest' material and 'funnies'. These clippings form the raw material from which the production team will construct 'News at Ten'. As games organiser, you should have one or two urgent news items up your sleeve (e.g. a statement on national security by the Prime Minister). These items are given to the production team at about

20 minutes and then 10 minutes before they are due to go 'on air', forcing changes to the 'running order' of news items .... this technique is nasty, but realistic, as it happens regularly in live news broadcasting.

Some props: a table and chairs for the presenters, and for journalists conducting interviews; materials to make a 'News at Ten' backdrop and captions if you have a very large group to keep occupied.

A Production Team:
Producer: 'the boss', answerable only to the games organiser. The producer co-ordinates the efforts of the entire production team, making sure that the programme goes out on time, etc.
Production Assistant: works out the running order of items and their length.
Editor: has the final say in the content of the programme.
Director: controls the artistic side of the production - cameras, captions, graphics, etc.
Journalists/presenters (2 at least): create 'copy' from the raw material available and present it to camera. Will also pre-record interviews (if a second video recorder is available).
Camera operator: checks that camera and microphone work properly and records any interviews and the final programme.
Props Team: responsible for all props (tables, chairs, etc.) and backdrops.
Electrician: responsible for camera lights (if in use).
Interviewees: for any pre-recorded interviews.
Cards with the various job descriptions written on them.
Depending on the size of the group you are working with you may only want to allocate the key roles, making sure that necessary tasks are re-allocated as appropriate.
Video recording and playback facilities. If you have a second video recorder and monitor, you can pre-record interviews which are then carefully slotted in as 'News at Ten' is presented. Even without a second recorder, you can still use the interview technique 'live', by getting the camera operator to 'pan' from the news presenter to the live interview as the programme is being recorded.

METHOD

Introduce the simulation to the group by telling them that in half an hour's time they will be presenting a live news broadcast!

Carefully go over the tasks and roles necessary to produce a news broadcast.

Now allocate roles to individuals, together with any materials, props, paper and pens they will need.

Stress that the production team has 30 **minutes only** to prepare the broadcast.

Remember to give the producer or editor the urgent news stories which are just 'breaking' (see above).

Give the group a countdown every 5 minutes, and then each minute for the final 5. Countdown the last 30 seconds to 'on air'.

'News at Ten' is now broadcasting 'live'.

DEBRIEFING

As this is a task-orientated simulation with a forced pace, the production team will have built up to a fast and furious level of action as 'on air' time approaches. Don't allow a break before recording, but keep the momentum going by moving straight into the presentation. Once it's recorded the production team will probably collapse with exhaustion. Call a short break now if you like, prior to watching the re-play of 'News at Ten', remembering to switch to your second playback machine for any pre-recorded interviews. You'll find that the group will analyse their performance and make comments during the re-play. Encourage this as a way of dissipating tension and give the group the opportunity of watching the replay again.

Issues you may wish to discuss include:

• What it feels like to be part of a task-oriented team creating a tangible 'product'.
• The need for leadership in this kind of situation.

• The quality of communication between participants. Role differentiation: does it need a different person to do each job?
• What would happen if there wasn't a producer, say, or an editor?
• Stress factors: which roles created most stress for people, and what was the effect?

Allow one to one and a half hours.

Notes.

Section Nine:
WORKING WITH
YOUNGER GROUPS

The existence of this section results from our contact with a number of friends and colleagues, and in particular, Lois Johnson.

THE NEEDS OF YOUNGER CHILDREN

Whilst all youngsters need caring and sensitive treatment, it is especially true of children in their pre-teens. They require the 'closeness' of adults and a heightened sense of 'belonging' to feel comfortable. In youth work, and indeed in family and friendship groups, younger children (roughly defined as under eleven or twelves) particularly enjoy the shared activity of games-playing. They respond to the freedom to experiment with their bodies and with language as powerful tools in personal development. Younger children enjoy activity and probably have fewer inhibitions about physical contact. In fact, their demands for such contact, even if it is expressed in boisterous and sometimes painful ways (well, how do you like your stomach being continuously pummelled?) are consistent with a quest for both attention and security.

GAMES PROGRAMMES

In introductory sessions, the following games from Section 2 of this book were found especially successful:

THE BALL GAME &
THE HELLO GAME..........*for getting to know one another*

ESCAPE/OUTSIDER &
TRUST IN A CIRCLE.........*as physical contact games*
THE FEET GAME

And from Section 6:

CATERPILLAR, TUNNEL TIG,
BATTLE BALL, UNI-HOC ....*energetic activity games*
DODGE BALL, FREEZE TAG

Workers with younger groups tend, rightly, like teachers in primary schools, to stress the value of co-operation and group cohesion. Lois, in using a range of games like 'Minister's Cat' and 'Pass the Squeeze' stressed the 'success' achieved by her groups in mastering the technique. Her club members successfully used 'Killer', but avoided using it with members under about eleven years old.

In addition to using a selective approach to the material contained in this book, you might wish to use ethnic, street-games such as British Bulldog and Piggy Back races, and even not-too-serious Piggy-Back fights! Other brief examples of good quick games are given in this section. They cover the complete range of situations in which games might be employed.

NAME SWAP
A quick way of introducing members to one another which stops the 'fidgets' in an energetic way. With the kids sitting in a circle, the leader shouts out 2 names and these two get up and race to change places. After a few rounds, the leader can ask a volunteer to re-start the sequence by calling out a name of another group member. They then run and change places.

JELLY
Tell the group that they must stand in a circle with their arms around one another. They are then instructed to imagine that they are a jelly on a plate wobbling from side to side. Lots of laughs and usually a 'spilled' jelly - all over the floor!

BLIND SNAKE CRAWL
Using scarves, or whatever comes to hand and is not too smelly, blindfold all the group members. The starting positions are at the outer edges of the room. Tell all the group members to crawl,

snake-fashion, (hissing, if they like!) round the room trying to locate each other. If your little snakes are getting lost, instruct them to ALL head for the centre of the room. A fine reptilian entanglement should result!

KIM'S GAME

We don't know who Kim is, or was, but that's the name of the game as far as we know! It is also sometimes known simply as 'Observation'.

The way the game works is to have a tray with about twenty objects on it. Everyone taking part must study the contents of the tray for one minute, or perhaps two minutes, with very young participants. The tray is then covered with a cloth and everyone is given a paper and pen and has to try and write down the names of all the objects they can remember. The winner is the person who gets most correct.

Obviously the game will not work if none of your group can write. It is also important to make sure that members of the group do **not** write down the objects while they are studying the tray.

PIG

We wanted to include card games which are not too familiar and we felt quite pleased with ourselves when we came across this one! The game is very well suited to younger groups as well as ageing adolescents like the writers! It is a game where inhibitions should be left outside and it should help to create a relaxed and laughter-filled environment.

You need a minimum of three players, and really five or six are the best sort of number. Thirteen players is the maximum, so you can almost use it as a party game!

The pack of cards needs to be sorted out into sets of four of a kind; four kings, four tens etc. You need to allocate four cards for each person playing. The cards are shuffled and each player is dealt four cards. Everyone looks at their four cards, with the aim of collecting a new set of four of a kind. Each player then places an unwanted card face down on the table and passes it to the player on their left. Once all the players have passed on a card, everyone looks again at their four cards to see if they have four of a kind.

Play continues in this way until one player has completed a set of four. And this is when the fun and havoc begin! To indicate that they have a set they should put a finger to their nose. Other players must pay attention to this since this is the signal for **all** the players to put a finger to their noses as well. The **last person to put a finger to their nose is the pig!**

The trick of playing the game is not to pay total attention to your own set, but instead keep a weather-eye open for other players pointing nosewards. Not a good game for playing with kids who pick their noses, perhaps!

JUMBLED NEWSPAPERS

We have found that this is a popular little game with younger groups of children. It also requires nothing more than a few newspapers for equipment. Ideally, each newspaper should be the same size, with the same number of pages. You need one newspaper for each participant.

The game sequence works like this. Each newspaper is jumbled up with the pages all in the wrong order. Each participant is handed out a newspaper and on the word 'go', each person has to try and sort out their newspaper into the correct order. The winner is the first person to have produced a paper back in its original order. Tabloid papers like the Mirror and the Mail are the best size to use-you never know some of the youngsters you play it with may even read the odd bit of their paper!

COCK FIGHTING

No, we don't condone blood-sports. It's just the name given to this particular physical game.

The equipment needed is one walking stick or broom handle for each contestant.
Each player crouches down on the floor facing an opponent, bringing their knees together under their chin. Their hands usually grip their knees as the stick or handle is passed over their arms and under their knees. Its easier to play than to describe in words, honestly!

The aim then is for one of the participants to topple the other over.

As a group activity, it tends to create a noisy audience response, so it cannot be played anywhere that youngsters have to be reasonably quiet. You've been warned!

MATCHBOX NOSES

This active sequence is a team game. The organiser must have a matchbox lid (the part without the matches in it!) for each team taking part. Teams line up in rows and on the command 'Start' or 'Go', the first person in each team places the matchbox lid on their nose. They then have to pass it on to the nose of the next person in the team line-without using hands and without anyone else helping or interfering. If any player drops the lid or it is touched with hands, then the lid must go back to the first person

in the line. The winning team is the first one to get the lid all the
way to the end of their line.

Lively fun, and a useful way to get group members working
together in teams.

NEWSPAPER WALK

This sequence is lively, active fun. It's very popular with all
younger groups and it's a good sequence for parties as well.
Mums and Dads and youth leaders etc. should all have a go - it's
not that easy! It is best played in a school hall or a scout hut,
where there is a shiny wooden floor.

Each player needs two sheets of newspaper. Players should have
taken their shoes off, otherwise the paper tends to rip. All the
participants line up, placing one sheet of newspaper under each
foot. At the word 'Start', players must try to cross the room
heading for the previously agreed finishing line. If any part of
player's body touches the floor, they have to go back to the start.

CLAP TRAP

Apparently this was originally a drinking game (how would we
know?). It uses rhythms and words. Get the group into a rhythm
of 2 claps, or stamps of the feet, followed by a pause. Once this
sequence is established, tell the group that they should think of
types of birds. In turn, each group member calls out a type of
bird. Successfully executed this sort of game is a good
confidence-builder. The topics are almost endless - flowers;
animals; fruits; colours etc.

MIME AND MOVEMENT

Mime and Movement techniques are particularly useful with
younger groups. Simple exercises using music to limber up are a
good way to start a session and to convey feelings and emotions
through movement and posture: fear; anger; strength etc. are
useful ways to introduce the world of body language.

RHUBARB

Derived from a silly 'Goon's' film, this sequence allows a 'volunteer' to try and convey meanings using only the word 'rhubarb', plus body actions to the group. It is good when played in pairs and the partner acting as spectator has to guess the meaning of the 'rhubarb'. Is it surprise? Are they cross? Hurt, perhaps? The list is almost endless.

SPECIAL EVENTS

Games can brighten up 'special' evenings for younger groups. We all know that they are the basis of birthday parties. They are just as useful in youth groups for Halloween; disco nights and special events.

From our experience, ducking for apples or treacle duffs; egg rolling; scavenger hunts and the use of quizzes all proved popular with younger members.

THE CHOCOLATE GAME

The next sequence proved almost universally popular wherever it was used!

A large block of chocolate is placed on a plate with a knife and fork. Scarf, hat and gloves lie close by. These items are situated in the centre of the circle of group members. The game commences with a dice being passed around quickly, each member having a turn with the dice. When a six is thrown, the successful player races into the middle, puts on hat, scarf and gloves and cuts a single square of chocolate from the block and starts eating. Eating continues for that player, single square at a time, until another six is thrown, then the clothes are passed on to the new chocolate-eater. Speed is the important thing. It's a great favourite.

BALLOON BURST

If you've played the party game where participants try to burst balloons, this is a bizarre variant. It's riotous and fun and not at all serious. The drawing Jerry has produced explains the sequence almost completely. Dave Bliss, a Yorkshireman who worked in

Govanhill, Glasgow, was responsible for the idea (all letters, hospital bills etc....to his new home in Northallerton).

The number of pairs involved is dependent upon the number of rubber lilo pumps available. Pairs are divided up and the smaller of each team is then sat on a pump on a chair. The teams start together, and the 'sitters' are lifted and dropped on their respective pumps until the balloons burst. Voluntary participation is recommended!

FINALLY ....

Leadership may be more important with younger groups. You will have to clearly state the rules before play commences and watch out for 'sulks' and unhappiness. Games are meant to be fun and you must be sensitive to any tensions which arise and try to alleviate anxiety as it occurs.

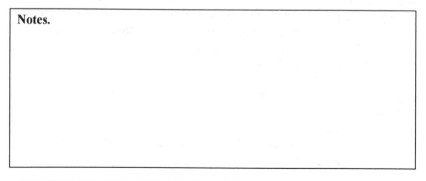

Notes.

Section Ten:
BIBLIOGRAPHY

Theory of Games

B. De Koven.
Interplay Games Catalogue.
(Intensive Learning Centre, 5th and Luzerne Street, Philadelphia.)

G. l. Gibbs.
Handbook of Games and Simulation Exercises
An extended bibliography, which must be treated with caution. With the speed of things changing in this arena, the collection is rather out of date. (E. & F. N. Spon, 1974)

Don Pavey and Michael Challinor.
The Art based Game as a mode of Education (1976) and the Art Arena Games Pack (1978) c/o School of Liberal Studies, Kingston Polytechnic, Penrhyn Road, Kingston, Surrey KT1 2EE.

S.A.G.S.E.T.
The Society for Academic Games and Simulations in Education and Training.
S.A.G.S.E.T., Centre for Extension Studies, University of Technology, Loughborough, Leicestershire.

D. Watts.
Simulations and Games with 'Less Able' Pupils; can be contacted through S.A.G.S.E.T.

History of Games

Arnold Arnold.
The World Book of Children's Games
Using historical principles, this games book concentrates on the younger age group and is best for reference in the sections on 'ball, bowling, beanbag and balloon games' and 'Strategic board games'.(Pan. 1976)

Michael Bentine and John Ennis.
Book of Square Games
The source of much mythical endeavour! (Wolfe Publishing 1966)

E. Berne.
Games People Play
A pleasing collection of psychological relationship games with some historical material. (Penguin 1970)

Edward de Bono.
The Five Day Course in Thinking
The originator of lateral thinking in a do-it-yourself guide. (Penguin 1972)
Edward de Bono.
The use of lateral thinking. (Pelican. 1971)
Edward de Bono.
Po: Beyond Yes and No. (Pelican. 1973)
Will Dexter.
The Illustrated Book of Magic Tricks.
A nicely presented and comprehensive collection of tricks and puzzles. Good on coins and cards. (Abbey Library. 1957)
Fleetway House.
Encyclopedia of Sports, Games and Pastimes.
A weighty, but interesting collection arranged alphabetically from acme skating to zoetropes. (Believed to have been published in 1935 by Fleetway House.)
Raymond Garman.
Games, Pastimes and Amusements: Indoor and Outdoor.
An American collection which is full of whimsy and old-fashioned party games. (Thompson and Thomas. 1900)
Alice B. Gomme.
The Traditional games of England, Scotland and Ireland.
Rather a tome and both academic and archaic. Good on singing and playground games. Originally published in two volumes in 1894 and 1898. (Thames and Hudson. 1984)
J. Strutt.
Sports and Pastimes of the People of England
A marvellous introduction to the history of British games. (First published 1801. Republished 1969 Firecrest Publishing)
Kenneth Wheeler.
The Handbook of Games and Pastimes.
With party games, board games, pub games and outdoor and travelling games, a useful collection. (Paul Hamlyn, 1963)

Relationship Games
Kevin Ball et al.
Worth The Risk.
A planned programme of material for structuring work with young offenders. It offers a structure to which much of the 'Youth Games Book' and 'The Gamesters Handbooks' can be attached. (SCF Hilltop and West Yorkshire Probation Service, 1987.)

Tim Bond.
Games for Social and Life Skills. A useful range of games and exercises is presented in a crisp, easy to use format. Good introductory section on the use of games. (Hutchinson Education, 1986.)

Blatner, H. B. (ed).
Acting in Practical Aspects of Psychodrama.
Informative and valuable as an introduction to this field of work with games.

D. Brandes and H. Phillips.
The Gamesters' Handbook. Each game is well described and aims, materials and variations are adequately explained. An excellent resource book! (Hutchinson 1977)

D. Brandes.
Gamesters 2.
Well thought out follow-up to 'The Gamesters' Handbook' with sections on All Purpose Games, Introductory Games and Group Leaders' Games. (Stanley Thorne. 1982)

Larry Butler and Lex Allison.
Games, Games.
A useful collection of cards, together with a short pamphlet/book on areas of use. The format is good; the material could do with more commentary regarding how the sequences work in different settings. (Playspace 1978)

J. Canfield and H. C. Wells
100 Ways to enhance self concept in the Classroom.
Aimed at teachers and parents, the book applies the Gestalt theory to teaching and offers a range of practical exercises through which kids can develop an understanding of themselves and a better self-image. (Prentice Hall 1976)

Cockpit Arts Workshop.
Warm-Ups and Ice Breakers.
A nicely produced large leaflet with many valuable games and role plays. (Alec Davison, Cockpit Arts workshop, Gateforth Street, London NW8 8EH).

Robin Dynes.
Creative Games in Group Work.
One of the best of the newer books on the use of games in social work, probation and group work with young people. Probably the best and most comprehensive book to use alongside the New Youth Games Book! (Winslow Press. 1990)

M. Harrison and the Non-Violent Children Program
For the Fun of It: Selected Co-operative games for Children and Adults. (1975)
A good collection and overlook at games in a co-operative setting.

Hoper, Claus-Kutzleb et. al.
Awareness Games.
Personal growth through group interaction.(St Martin's Press, 1975 translated into

English).An early and very useful collection of games and sequences, together with 'points to watch for'. Well organised.

Martin Jelfs.

Manual for Action.

An activist's stance on getting things done and speeding up change, this manual embodies theory and practical exercises for non-violent training and group learning. Some sessions, like the 'group massage' may be deemed unsuitable for youth groups! (Action Resources Group, 1982.)

Kingston Friends' Workshop Group.

Ways & Means: An approach to problem solving.

An A4 ringbound collection of workshop material for working in schools and with youth groups. Some unusual material collected from overseas. (Kingston Friends. 1985)

Daphne Lennox.

Residential Group Therapy for Children. Offers examples of transactional analysis techniques and sequences. (Tavistock Publications, 1982.)

Leslie Lawson.

Lead On.

Youth leadership-US of A style! An interesting introduction to a very different culture.

Elice Milroy.

Role Play.

A useful guide to the use of role plays in a variety of settings. (Aberdeen University Press.1982)

Simon Myhill.

Drama.

An excellent little handbook giving thorough coverage of the use of drama and role play with groups of young people. Very practical and informative with lots of ideas, techniques and exercises. Recommended. (National Association of Youth Clubs, 1975.)

National Youth Agency.

Leap Confronting Conflict.

A training course outline on dealing with conflict, which has a number of useful games and sequences. (National Youth Agency)

Panmure House.

'So You Think You Can Play Games?'

A Handbook of Group Games and Techniques. (Panmure House 1978)

This was the 'bible' for relationship games, but the nasty I.T. Resource Centre (us) gobbled their material and included it in sections 4 and 5.

Christine Poulter.
Playing the Game.
From a drama background, role plays and introductory games sequences. A bit poor relative to Dynes or Brandes. (Macmillan.1987)
Remocker/Storch.
Action Speaks Louder.
A handbook of non-verbal group techniques. An interesting collection used by occupational therapists. Detailed and well presented. (Churchill Livingstone, 1982.)

Indoor Games, Puzzles and Travelling Games

Alfred Aleut.
Within Doors.
A Victorian collection of: "games and pastimes for the drawing room." Good on puzzles with string and card tricks. (T.Nelson. 1872)
R. C. Bell.
Board and Table Games
A comprehensive, if rather stodgy collection of board games, it gives little idea of how valuable one game is compared with another. Perhaps they hadn't tried them ! (offstage cries of "heresy").(O. U. P. Vol.1 1960 and Vol.11 1969)
Gyles Brandreth.
The Hamlyn Family Games Book
One of the "what you can do on a journey or wet day" variety. Intelligently put together, as befits the author, though a little thin on the content. There's a good puzzle section at the back which we photocopied and used with groups. Yet another copyright infringement! (Hamlyn paperback 1978)
Gyles Brandreth.
Indoor Games.
Well organised as a collection, the material covered echoes some of the sections in this book. You may find one or two new Parlour Games. (Teach Yourself Books 1977).
Gyles Brandreth.
Brandreth's Bedroom Book.
Described as providing something other than sex and sleep for the bedroom! An oddly mixed book of diversions for the insomniac! (Eyre Methuen. 1973)
Maxey Brooke.
Coin games and puzzles
Really rather a boring, self-opinionated presentation, but it does include some original games and puzzles. (Constable 1973)
Jonathan Cape.
100 Amazing Magic Tricks.
Published in Britain in 1977. Translated from a turn of the century French tome, this

collection is visually uplifted by original lithographs. Many are impossible to build; lots are hazardous, but the whole publication fascinates most teenage readers.
Ann Cole et al.
A pumpkin in a pear tree.
A parents and teachers' holiday activity book from America, which includes many unusual games. (Little, Brown & Co. 1976)
The Diagram Group.
The Way to Play - The Illustrated Encyclopaedia of the Games of the World.
An amazing book in every sense of the word. We found it invaluable and there's still plenty of fascinating material for you to browse through. The diagrams are faultless, the coverage is as near comprehensive as is humanly possible, and the rules are, in the main, clearly explained. (Bantam 1977)
Joseph Edmunson.
The Best Party Games.
Provides a comprehensive range of party games for all ages and situations like Beach Parties, barbecues etc.(illustrated Pan Books)
Martin Gardner.
Mathematical Puzzles and Diversions
Only to be dipped into for youth work use. Most of the contents are far too esoteric. (Penguin 1961 & companion volumes)
Eve Harlow.
101 Instant Games.
Nicely illustrated and a varied collection. Some of the games' descriptions are rather brief, but Larry's cartoons do wonders for the presentation. Worth having a look at. (1977 MacDonald).
Know the Game.
Inn Games.
A short compilation of games from the smoke filled back bar of your local! (Educational Productions. 1955)
Vladimir Kozian.
Mazes. If you are looking for something different to leave around, this might be it! Used with tracing paper or photocopied, the book itself could last some while. The contents are mostly quite difficult, so the result of frustration might be a shredded book! (Pan 1972).
Marshall Cavandish
The Bumper Fun Book.
With 365 things-to-do, this is the most interesting, well presented collection that we have come across. Good for 10+ age group. Recommended.
Jerome Meyer
Puzzle Quiz and Stunt Fun

(Dover Publications USA). An old-fashioned collection of puzzles and party items. Dated, but still of some interest. (Marshall Cavendish. 1978)

David Parlett.
Penguin Book of Card Games.
Ours is a hardback copy. It's very detailed and comprehensive. (Allen Lane. 1979)

Tony Potter.
Travel Games.
Well illustrated collection of games, puzzles and activities for youthful travellers and their adults! (Usborne 1986)

Hubert Phillips.
Pan Book of Card Games Old fashioned, yet quite satisfactory as a collection. As a complementary source to the Way to Play, it can be a useful item to prop up the bookshelves. (Pan 1960)

Ronald Ridout.
Puzzles Galore
For younger kids, it is a fill-in-the-missing picture/sentence variety of book. Not bad. (Dragon Books 1976)

Donald Sapsford.
Card Games and Patience.
Exactly what it says, aimed very much at children. (Starfish Books. Undated)

Richard Sharp & David Pritchard.
Christmas Crackers
Lots of quick puzzles, games, card games and patience. (Sunday Times, Xmas 1979)

Alfred Sheinwold.
101 Best Card Games for Children.
Dated, but contains some unusual games created by the author. (Nicholas Kaye. 1958)

Arthur Taylor.
Pub Games. A valuable collection of the normal and the odd, many of which we have usefully used in the youth and social work setting. Amusingly written and readable as a whole. (Mayflower Books 1976)

Group and Activity Games

Jack Cox.
Fun and games outdoors.
Quite a useful collection for people organising playschemes and holiday courses, or just wanting ideas for fun on the beach. (Pan. 1971)

A. Fluegelman.
The New Games Book

Well produced, and overall a human and readable collection of alternative games you can use with groups of youngsters and adults ranging in size from 2 to a collossal 1,300 in the case of the Lap Sit record! Recommended. (Sidgwick and Jackson 1976)

Camilla Nightingale.
Who Am I?
A handbook of techniques and exercises, designed for photo-copying, which encourages young people to develop skills of self-assessment and understanding of their own lives and relationships. (Jacquis Publishing, 1986).

T. Orlick.
The Co-operative Sports and Games Book.
Mostly for younger children under twelve, but some of the material can be used in a mixed age setting. (Writers and Readers Publishing Co-op.1979 Britain)

Alan Smith.
Working Out of Doors with Young People
A lively set of practical exercises for use with all types of youth groups in the great outdoors, ranging from street orienteering to obstacle races and canoeing. Now, sadly out of print. (Scottish I.T.R.C.1987)

Robin Smith.
Body Games.
An odd collection with some nice illustrations. Sub-titled: Challenging diversions, it includes icebreakers, new games and body-puzzles without ever calling them that! (Cedar Press. 1988)

Nigel Viney and Neil Grant.
Ball Games.
An illustrated history of balls games from all over the world. (Book Club Associates. 1978)

Weinsteen and Goodman.
Playfair, everybody's guide to non-competitive play
A good companion to 'The New Games Book'. (Impact Publishers, 1980)

Alexander Van Rensalaer.
Party Games.
Over 200 party games. (Panther. 1965.)

Younger Groups

Roger Hope and colleagues.
Kids!
An excellent source book for those working with younger kids. The booklet includes dozens of useful games in addition to a wide coverage of other worthwhile group activities. Possibly no longer available. (NAYC)

Simulations

Sarane S. Bookock and E. Schild.
Simulation Games in Learning.
(See especially Dale Farran's section 'Competition and Learning for underachievers'.)
One of the early writings on games which is a part of the academic backdrop to the
New Games era. (Sage California 1968)
Alec Davison and Peter Gordon.
Games and Simulations in Action.
Simulation in the educational setting would be a better title. Most useful for Youth
Social Work is the section on the making of Simulations.(Woburn Press 1978)

Notes.

AND IT'S AU REVOIR FROM US!!!!

We hope you've enjoyed the NEW YOUTH GAMES BOOK.

We've always felt that games have a bit of magic to offer to young people,
and to some who are not so young! The current collection has evolved over
many years. Some we learned when we were kids; some featured in our
daily lives as youth club leader - teacher - youth social worker, and some
are recent acquaintances and are included in this ever-evolving collection
for the first time.

Do contact us through Russell House Publishing if you have any ideas for
games we might try out, or consider for future compendiums. Likewise, if
you can't make a sequence work, or you want us to come and organise a
games training session for your staff team, drop us a line.

Have Fun - Happy Games Playing!

Alan + Howie
Alan & Howie